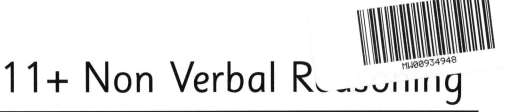

11+ Non Verbal Reasoning

The
Non-Verbal Ninja
Training Course

Book 1
Sequences

CEM-style Practice Exam Paper Questions
with *Visual* Explanations

Eureka! Eleven Plus Exams

The Eureka! 11+ Confidence series
CEM-style Practice Exam Papers covering:
Comprehension, Verbal Reasoning,
Non-Verbal Reasoning and Numerical Reasoning

Numerical Reasoning: Advanced Training Workbooks

Tough exam paper questions and detailed explanations of how to tackle them, to increase speed and reduce error.

Verbal Reasoning: Advanced Training Workbooks
The *1000-Word Brain Boost* is a powerful, intensive course teaching Synonyms, Antonyms, Odd-One-Out, Analogy, Vocabulary and Cloze in CEM-style questions. Its famous *Explanations* section explains hundreds of language subtleties and distinctions that many 11+ candidates find challenging.

Non-Verbal Reasoning: The *Non-Verbal Ninja* Training Course
The *Non-Verbal Ninja* is an intensive *visual* course for core CEM exam skills. The 3 training workbooks include over 600 puzzles coupled with *visual* explanations. They build both fundamental skills and the crucial confidence to seek out rules without having to have them explained first. Each book rapidly moves on from simple levels to challenging training puzzles that enhance the capacities of even the strongest 11+ hopefuls.

Please check the website www.eureka11plus.org/updates for updates and clarifications for this book.

Copyright © Eureka! Eleven Plus Exams 2016
Best-selling, realistic, 11+ exam preparation series

Publication date: January 2016
First published in the United Kingdom by Eureka! Eleven Plus Exams
http://www.eureka11plus.org   ·   Email: office@eureka11plus.org

ISBN-13: 978-1522932994
ISBN-10: 1522932992

We are all human and vulnerable to error. Eureka! Eleven Plus is very grateful to any reader who notifies us on office@eureka11plus.org of an unnoticed error, so we can immediately correct it and provide a tangible reward.

Non-Verbal Ninja

Non-verbal reasoning questions in the 11+ exam provoke anxiety amongst students and parents alike, since the test seems, at first, to be unlike the activities of normal everyday life. In reality, however, it is straightforward to train to improve one's performance in these puzzles.

The *Non-Verbal Ninja Training Course* from Eureka! Eleven Plus Exams is a three-part series of training books with several features to maximise the skill boost they provide to students.

- Full explanations are given immediately after each block of questions

- **Visual explanations** are provided where these are easier to understand

- The early questions of each type are easy, testing only one or two rules

- Challenging, broad-ranging questions are soon introduced

- Each question teaches an additional skill or reinforces a core skill

- You are **not** told in advance exactly what the rule will be, so you build confidence in identifying the rule for yourself — a crucial skill for exam success

The series of books, studied in sequence, covers the spectrum of types of format of questions and of the types of rule being tested. Some rules can be tested in many different settings.

Dedicated practice and, more importantly, careful review of the explanations of questions that turned out to be difficult, is the key to success in Non-Verbal Reasoning.

Become an 11+ Non-Verbal Ninja!

To gain the most from this course, follow the path of success

Focus on learning as many new rules as possible

Look forward to finding many questions you cannot answer correctly at first, as these are what make the training worthwhile

Expect the first few questions of each type to be easy

Do not skip ahead if questions seem easy. Each is building up your experience which you may need to draw upon for later questions. The questions quickly become more difficult.

While training, spend as much time as you need

The Ninja Training Course is not a race. Savour the learning and be enriched by it. The longer you spend thinking about all possible solutions to a problem, the more you will learn when the explanation is revealed.

Bite size

If you are studying in short chunks of time, plan ahead so that you have time to *review the explanations*. For example, if you only have a few minutes, you might tackle one page and carefully read the answers and explanations for it.

"I give up"?

Top ninjas don't just give up. They learn from challenging questions by writing a list of rules that they tried, and why they didn't work. Strike out the options that you know to be wrong, and indicate why. This could be diagrammatically, as you see in the answer pages. The more care you put into these baffling questions, the more you will learn from the explanation, and the more easily you will recognise this rule in the only questions that really matter – the ones in the exam.

Work steadily through the books of the course

The principles in book 1 are applicable throughout the training course, as they can be tested in many types of question.

Practice entire papers

Entire exam papers consist of non-verbal reasoning questions mixed in with other types. Use the *11+ Confidence* family of Practice Exam Papers to build your experience of this variety.

Training Session 1

In each question, look at the three cells and decide which of the six options A-F would best complete the sequence. Circle the single best option.

These first steps on your journey to excellence in the Non-Verbal Ninja Training Course. You will learn to be comfortable recognising patterns without being told in advance what they will be, since this is the situation you will face in the exam.

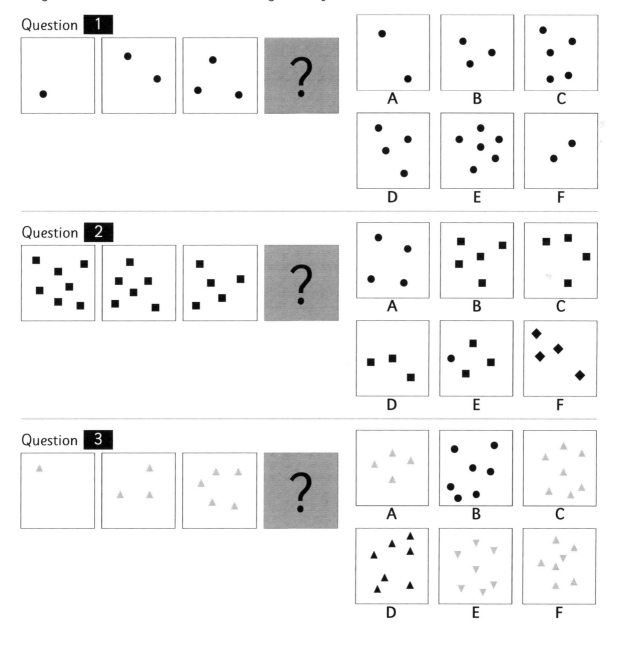

Go to the next page ➡

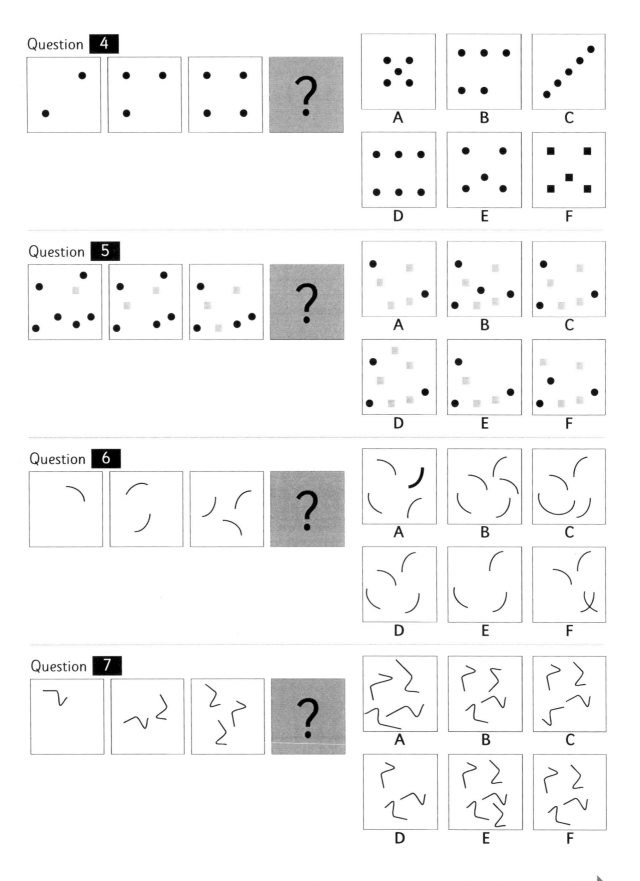

Question 4

Question 5

Question 6

Question 7

Go to the next page

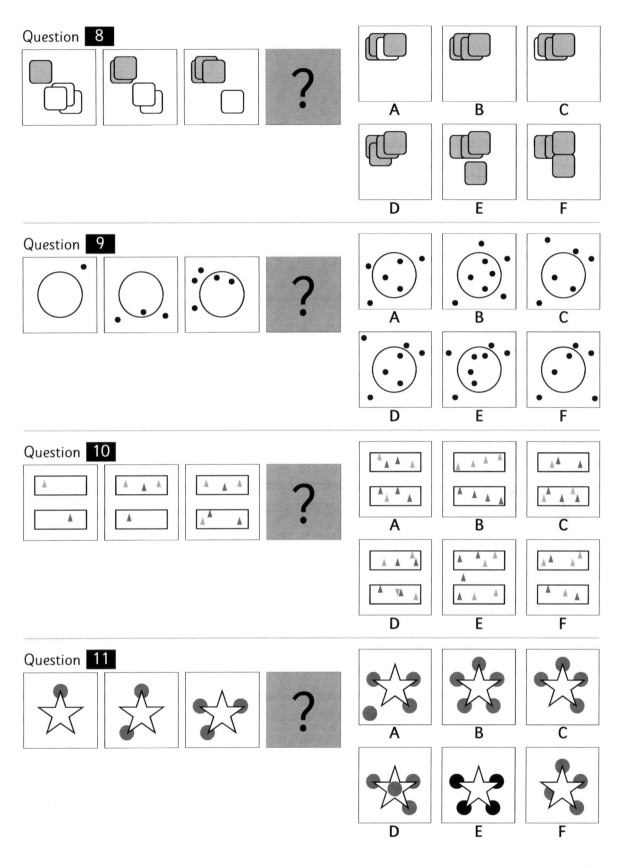

Question 8

Question 9

Question 10

Question 11

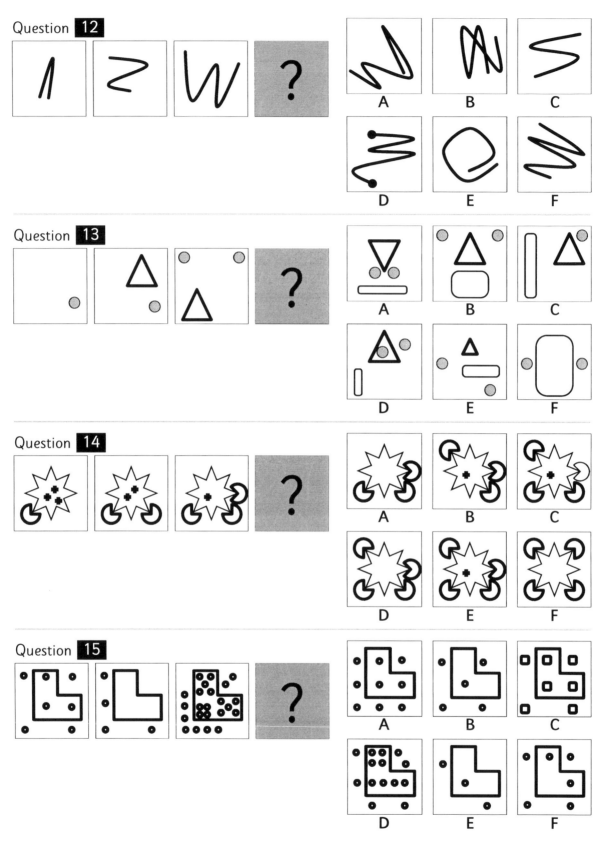

This is the end of this session.

Answers to Session 1

This training session taught many ways that a **counting** rule can be applied. You may have found much of this first Training Session easy.

Below we have boxed the correct answer cell. Examine the explanations to learn the reasons for the answers. The explanation is partly written under the question cells and partly (where this is easier to understand) drawn directly onto the answer options.

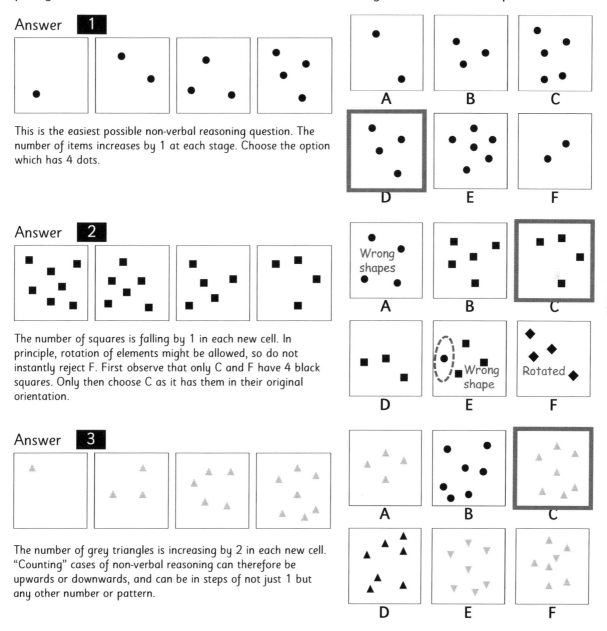

Answer 1

This is the easiest possible non-verbal reasoning question. The number of items increases by 1 at each stage. Choose the option which has 4 dots.

Answer 2

The number of squares is falling by 1 in each new cell. In principle, rotation of elements might be allowed, so do not instantly reject F. First observe that only C and F have 4 black squares. Only then choose C as it has them in their original orientation.

Answer 3

The number of grey triangles is increasing by 2 in each new cell. "Counting" cases of non-verbal reasoning can therefore be upwards or downwards, and can be in steps of not just 1 but any other number or pattern.

Go to the next page

Answer 4

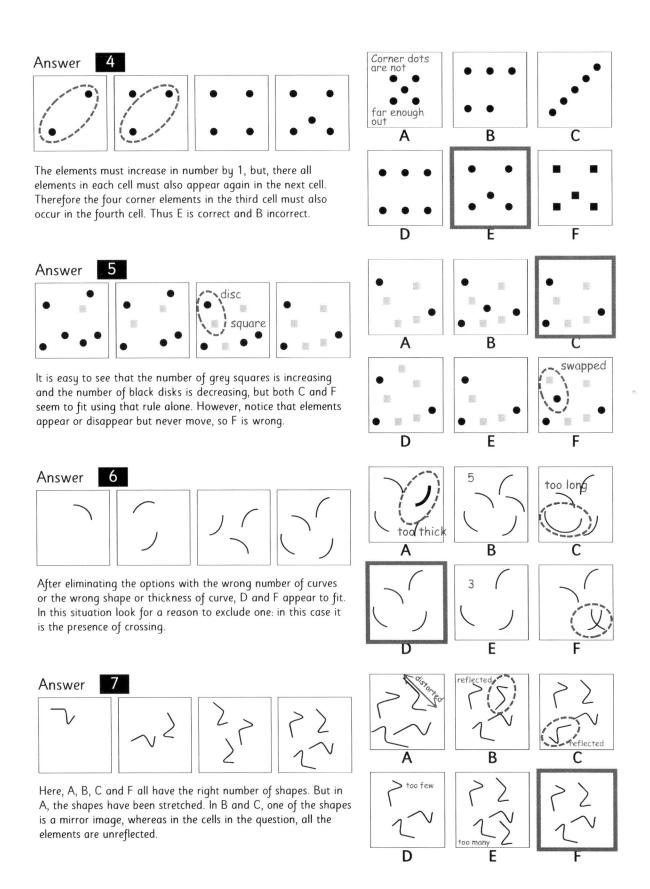

The elements must increase in number by 1, but, there all elements in each cell must also appear again in the next cell. Therefore the four corner elements in the third cell must also occur in the fourth cell. Thus E is correct and B incorrect.

Answer 5

It is easy to see that the number of grey squares is increasing and the number of black disks is decreasing, but both C and F seem to fit using that rule alone. However, notice that elements appear or disappear but never move, so F is wrong.

Answer 6

After eliminating the options with the wrong number of curves or the wrong shape or thickness of curve, D and F appear to fit. In this situation look for a reason to exclude one: in this case it is the presence of crossing.

Answer 7

Here, A, B, C and F all have the right number of shapes. But in A, the shapes have been stretched. In B and C, one of the shapes is a mirror image, whereas in the cells in the question, all the elements are unreflected.

Go to the next page ▶

Answer 8

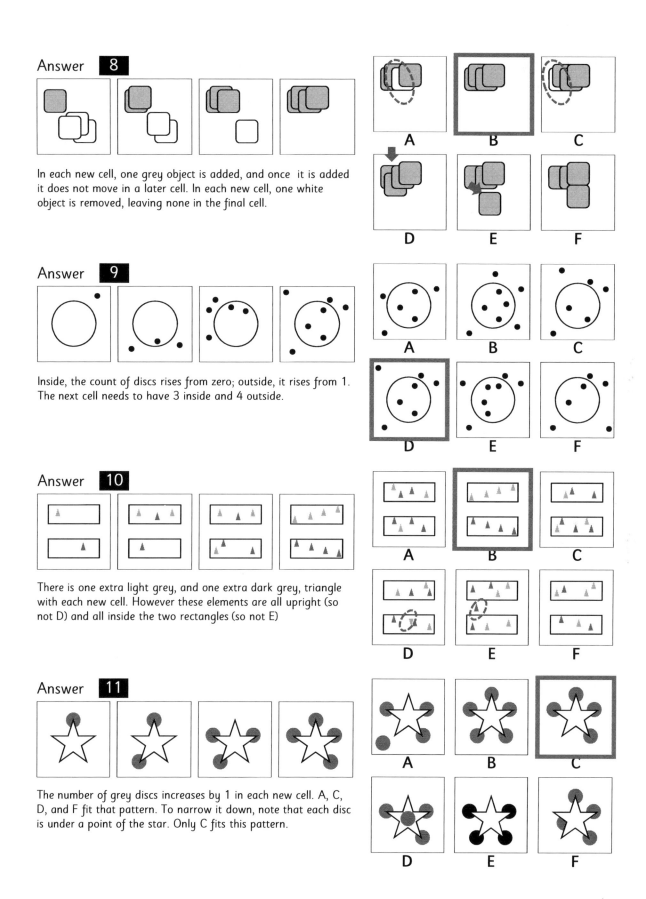

In each new cell, one grey object is added, and once it is added it does not move in a later cell. In each new cell, one white object is removed, leaving none in the final cell.

Answer 9

Inside, the count of discs rises from zero; outside, it rises from 1. The next cell needs to have 3 inside and 4 outside.

Answer 10

There is one extra light grey, and one extra dark grey, triangle with each new cell. However these elements are all upright (so not D) and all inside the two rectangles (so not E)

Answer 11

The number of grey discs increases by 1 in each new cell. A, C, D, and F fit that pattern. To narrow it down, note that each disc is under a point of the star. Only C fits this pattern.

Go to the next page

Answer 12

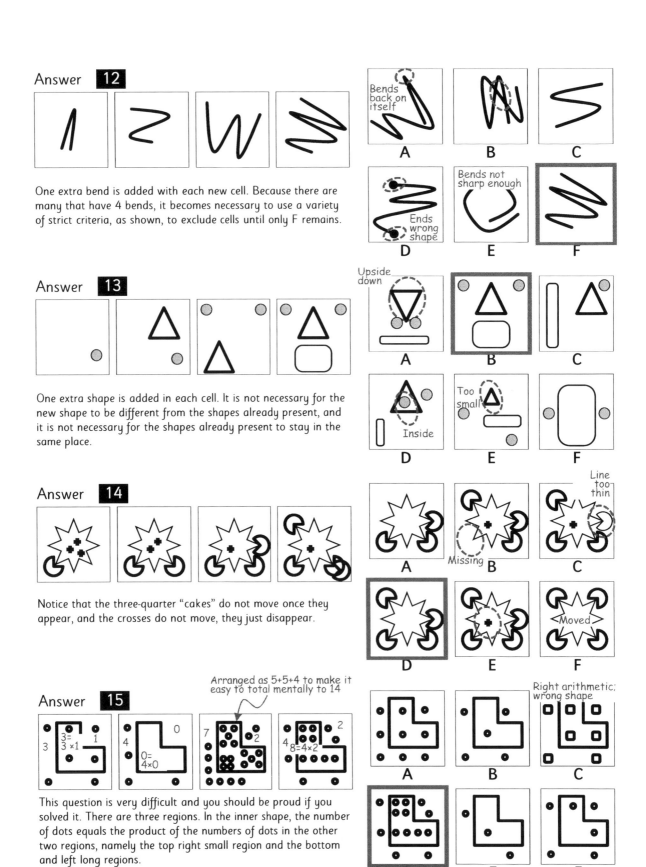

One extra bend is added with each new cell. Because there are many that have 4 bends, it becomes necessary to use a variety of strict criteria, as shown, to exclude cells until only F remains.

Bends back on itself — A
B
C
Ends wrong shape — D
Bends not sharp enough — E
F

Answer 13

One extra shape is added in each cell. It is not necessary for the new shape to be different from the shapes already present, and it is not necessary for the shapes already present to stay in the same place.

Upside down — A
B
C
Inside — D
Too small — E
F

Answer 14

Notice that the three-quarter "cakes" do not move once they appear, and the crosses do not move, they just disappear.

A
Missing — B
Line too thin — C
D
E
Moved — F

Answer 15

Arranged as 5+5+4 to make it easy to total mentally to 14

This question is very difficult and you should be proud if you solved it. There are three regions. In the inner shape, the number of dots equals the product of the numbers of dots in the other two regions, namely the top right small region and the bottom and left long regions.

A
B
Right arithmetic; wrong shape — C
D
E
F

12

This is the end of this session.

Training Session 2

You are now skilled in the "counting" aspect of non-verbal reasoning questions. Now tackle questions with another aspect. This new aspect will not be described: you will build your understand of it step-by-step through experience, and then review the full explanations in the answers. Watch out for questions that include "counting", since in the real exam you will not be told which question type each question is.

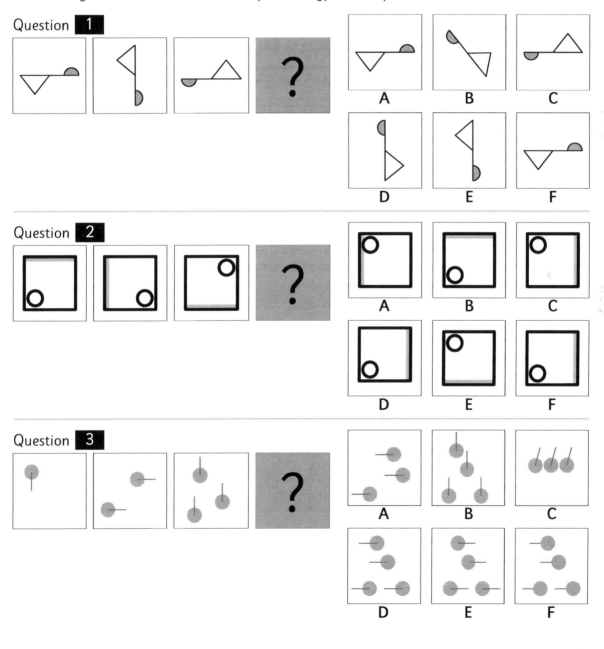

Go to the next page

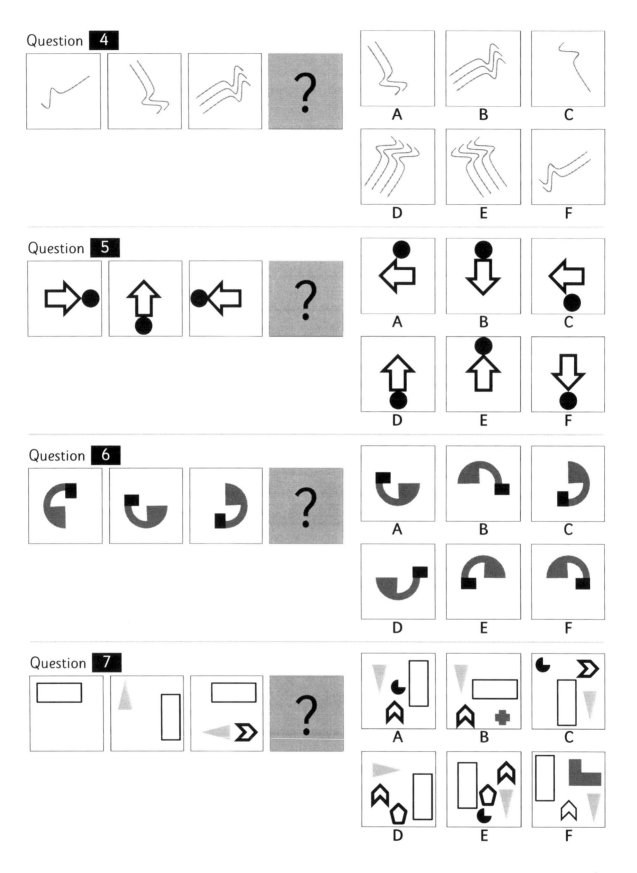

Go to the next page

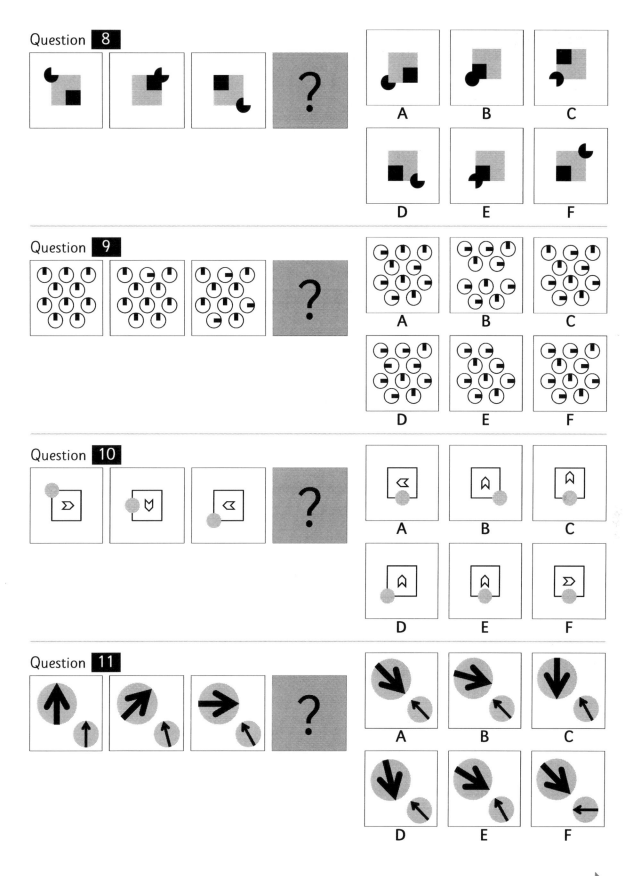

Go to the next page

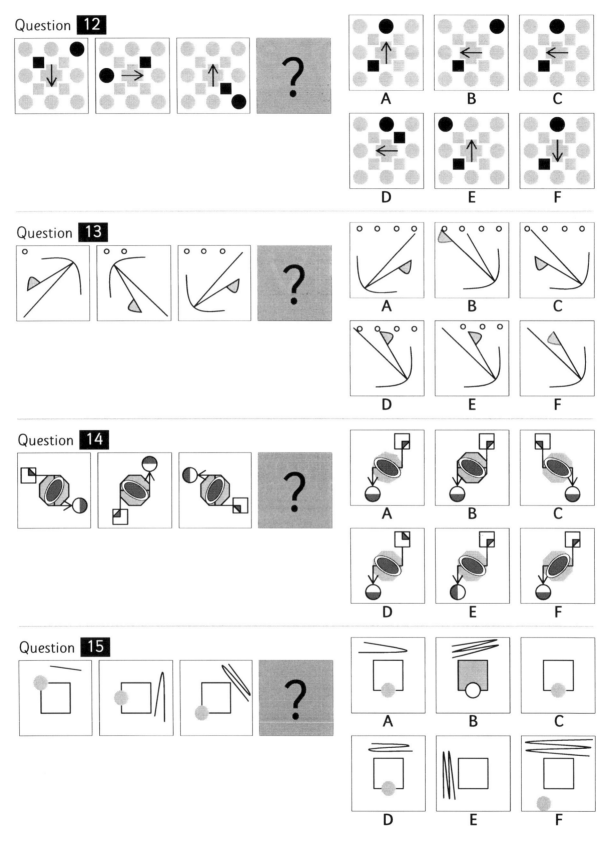

This is the end of this session.

Rotation   In this training session you began with a simple example of the pattern of rotation, and then built experience with more complex cases, intermingling them with cases of counting, either alone or combined with rotation. These training sessions are a tried and proven strategy to help you build the necessary experience of recognising what patterns are being tested, and making you confident to deduce new patterns for yourself.

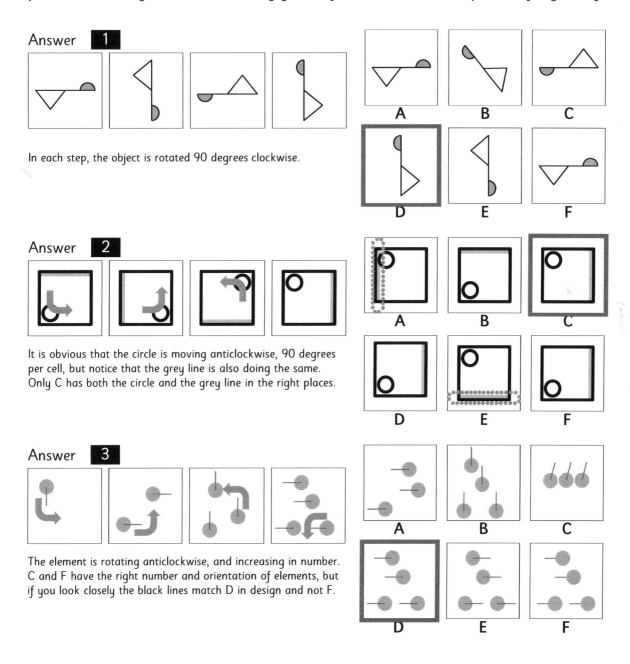

Answer 1

In each step, the object is rotated 90 degrees clockwise.

Answer 2

It is obvious that the circle is moving anticlockwise, 90 degrees per cell, but notice that the grey line is also doing the same. Only C has both the circle and the grey line in the right places.

Answer 3

The element is rotating anticlockwise, and increasing in number. C and F have the right number and orientation of elements, but if you look closely the black lines match D in design and not F.

Go to the next page ➡

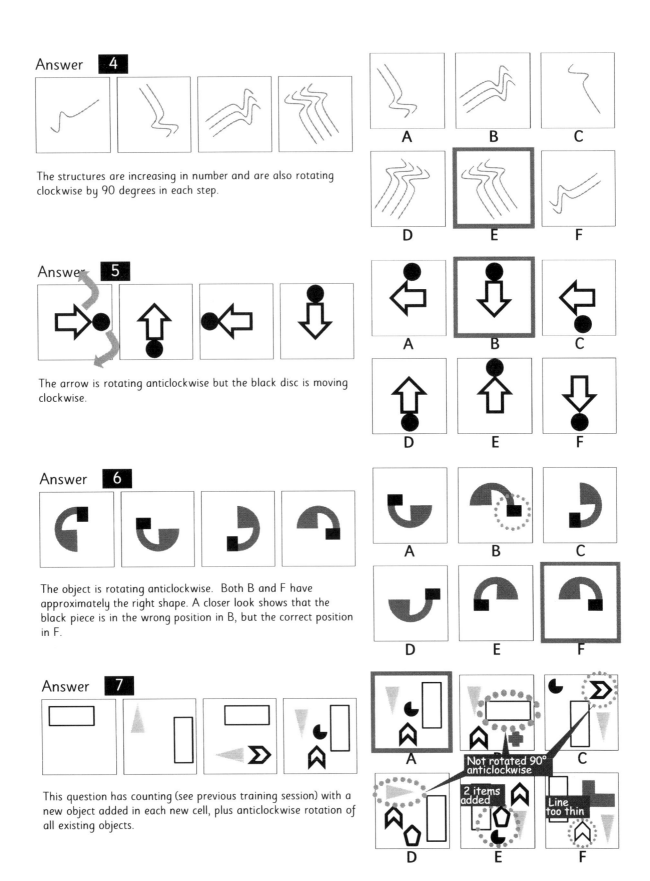

Answer 4

The structures are increasing in number and are also rotating clockwise by 90 degrees in each step.

Answer 5

The arrow is rotating anticlockwise but the black disc is moving clockwise.

Answer 6

The object is rotating anticlockwise. Both B and F have approximately the right shape. A closer look shows that the black piece is in the wrong position in B, but the correct position in F.

Answer 7

This question has counting (see previous training session) with a new object added in each new cell, plus anticlockwise rotation of all existing objects.

Not rotated 90° anticlockwise

2 items added

Line too thin

Go to the next page ➡

Answer 8

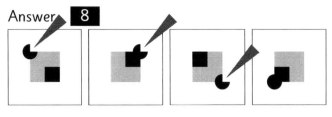

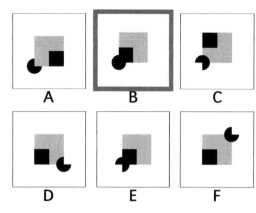

The grey square (with a black square inside) is rotating anticlockwise. There is a small black "¾ cake" shape moving clockwise in front of the square. Look carefully: the gap in the ¾ cake always remains to the top right.

Answer 9

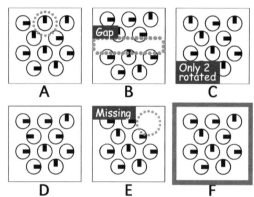

Counting and rotation Each cell contains the same 10 elements, with some elements rotated 90° clockwise from one cell to the next. From the 1st cell to the 2nd, one element rotates (and remains rotated for all future cells). From the 2nd cell to the 3rd, 2 more elements rotate. So from the 3rd to the 4th, 3 more elements rotate.

Answer 10

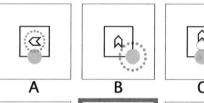

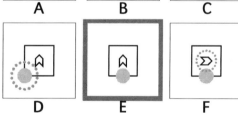

The grey disc is moving anticlockwise. However this is not by a ¼ turn per cell, but a 1/8 turn per cell. Meanwhile the chevron in the middle is rotating clockwise ¼ turn per cell.

Answer 11

The big arrow turns 45° per cell. You know this because two steps turn it 90°, from up to right. So next it will point 45° down and right, i.e. perfectly diagonally in the square. Only A and F show this and F clearly has turned its small arrow too much.

Go to the next page ➡

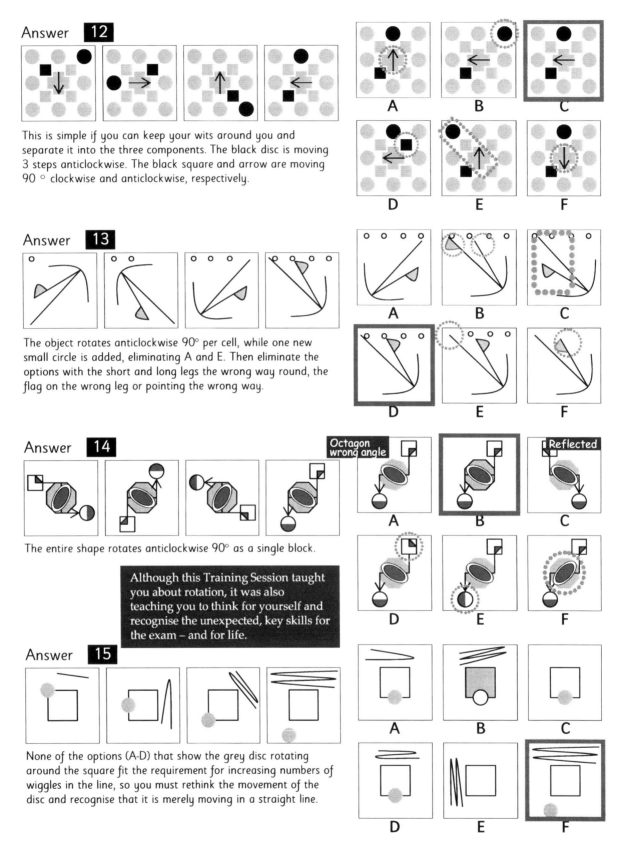

Answer 12

This is simple if you can keep your wits around you and separate it into the three components. The black disc is moving 3 steps anticlockwise. The black square and arrow are moving 90 ° clockwise and anticlockwise, respectively.

Answer 13

The object rotates anticlockwise 90° per cell, while one new small circle is added, eliminating A and E. Then eliminate the options with the short and long legs the wrong way round, the flag on the wrong leg or pointing the wrong way.

Answer 14

The entire shape rotates anticlockwise 90° as a single block.

Although this Training Session taught you about rotation, it was also teaching you to think for yourself and recognise the unexpected, key skills for the exam – and for life.

Answer 15

None of the options (A-D) that show the grey disc rotating around the square fit the requirement for increasing numbers of wiggles in the line, so you must rethink the movement of the disc and recognise that it is merely moving in a straight line.

This is the end of this session. ✖

Training Session 3

Now the range of rules applied broadens even wider. Use the ninja skills you have already acquired and look for new types of rule.

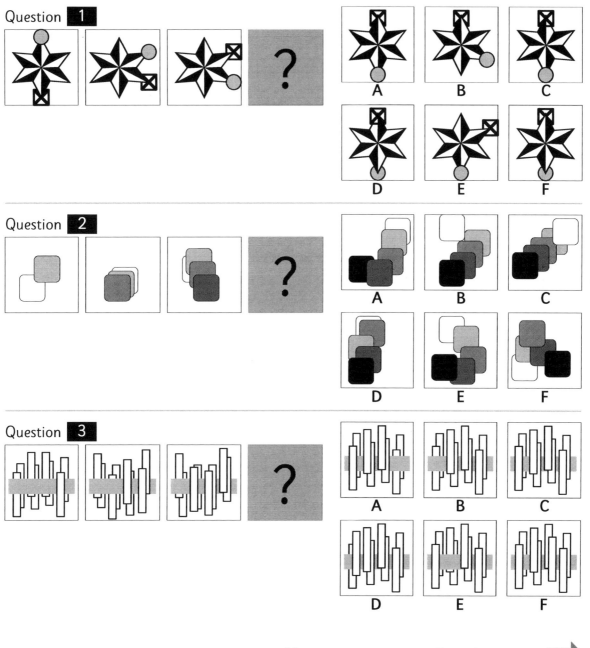

Question 1

Question 2

Question 3

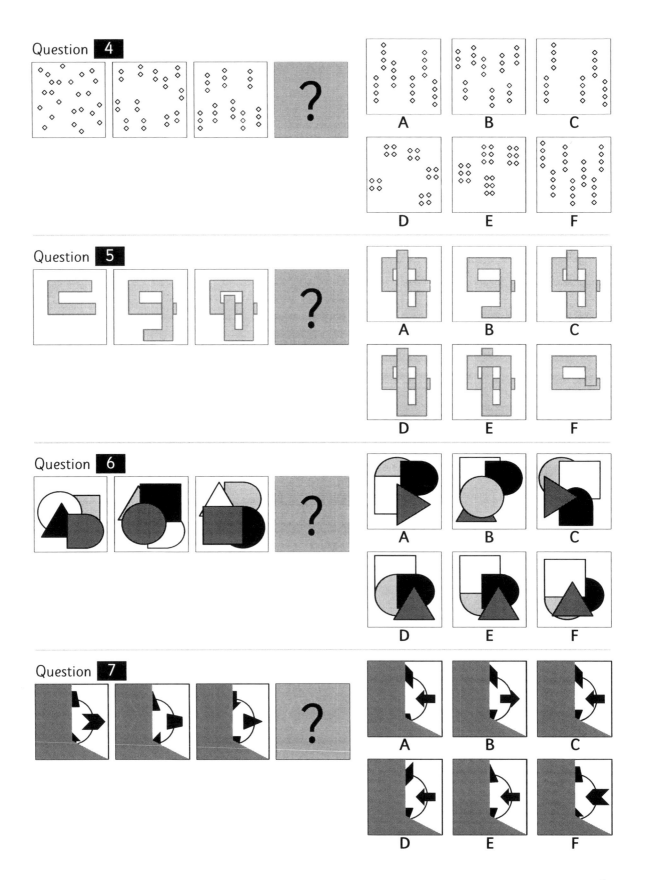

Go to the next page

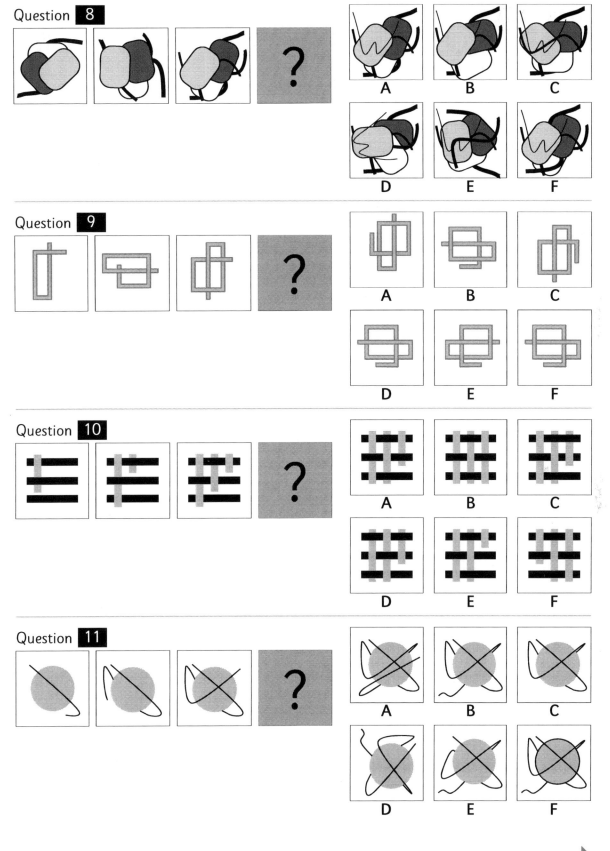

Question 8

Question 9

Question 10

Question 11

23

Go to the next page

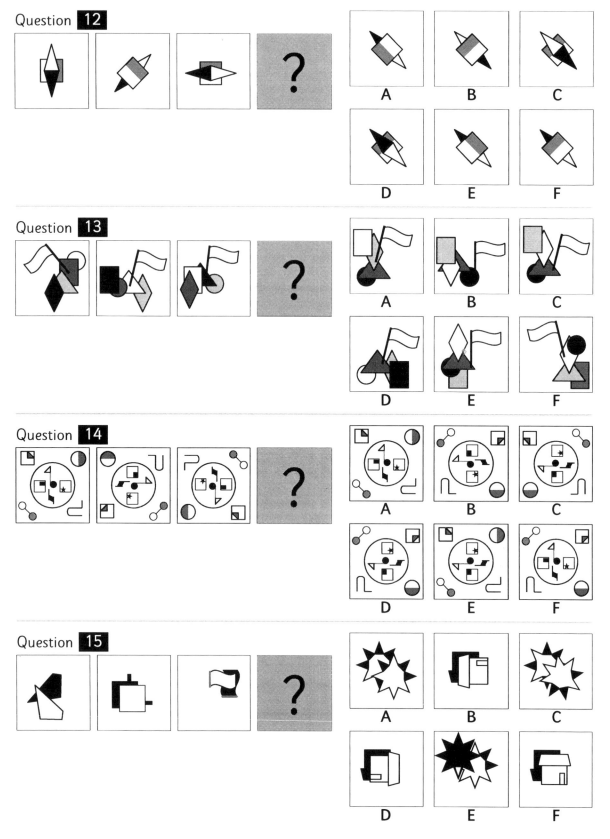

Question **12**

Question **13**

Question **14**

Question **15**

This is the end of this session.

Answers to Session 3

Your ninja skills have now increased to include handling overlapping **layers**, and examining levels of **shading**. The habit of recognising new types of rule without having them described to you immediately before is vital to success in Non-Verbal Reasoning questions, since they test mental agility.

Answer **1**

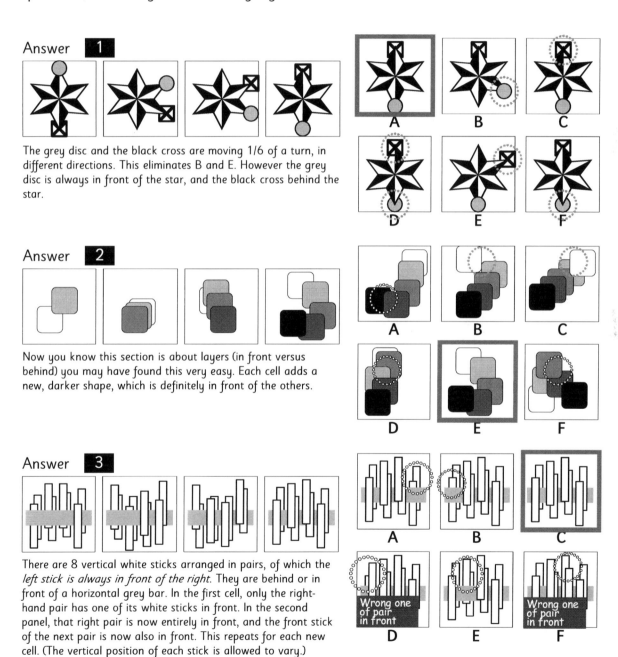

The grey disc and the black cross are moving 1/6 of a turn, in different directions. This eliminates B and E. However the grey disc is always in front of the star, and the black cross behind the star.

Answer **2**

Now you know this section is about layers (in front versus behind) you may have found this very easy. Each cell adds a new, darker shape, which is definitely in front of the others.

Answer **3**

There are 8 vertical white sticks arranged in pairs, of which the *left stick is always in front of the right*. They are behind or in front of a horizontal grey bar. In the first cell, only the right-hand pair has one of its white sticks in front. In the second panel, that right pair is now entirely in front, and the front stick of the next pair is now also in front. This repeats for each new cell. (The vertical position of each stick is allowed to vary.)

Go to the next page ➡

Answer 4

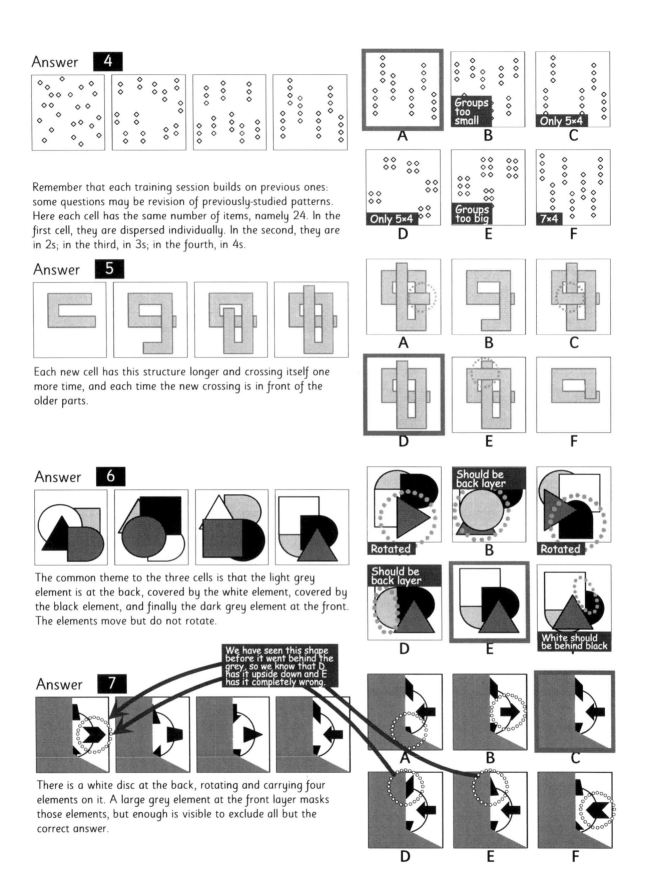

Remember that each training session builds on previous ones: some questions may be revision of previously-studied patterns. Here each cell has the same number of items, namely 24. In the first cell, they are dispersed individually. In the second, they are in 2s; in the third, in 3s; in the fourth, in 4s.

Answer 5

Each new cell has this structure longer and crossing itself one more time, and each time the new crossing is in front of the older parts.

Answer 6

The common theme to the three cells is that the light grey element is at the back, covered by the white element, covered by the black element, and finally the dark grey element at the front. The elements move but do not rotate.

Answer 7

There is a white disc at the back, rotating and carrying four elements on it. A large grey element at the front layer masks those elements, but enough is visible to exclude all but the correct answer.

Go to the next page ➡

Answer 8

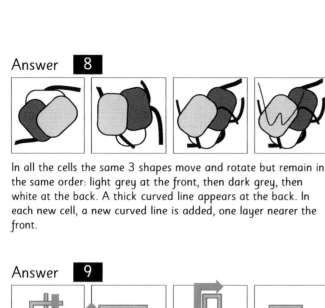

In all the cells the same 3 shapes move and rotate but remain in the same order: light grey at the front, then dark grey, then white at the back. A thick curved line appears at the back. In each new cell, a new curved line is added, one layer nearer the front.

Answer 9

In each new cell, the shape lengthens and crosses itself one more time, *alternating between in front versus behind* the previous parts of the shape. The shape is rotating clockwise. To check the orientation easily, draw a big, asymmetrical, "L" on the first bend of the shape.

Answer 10

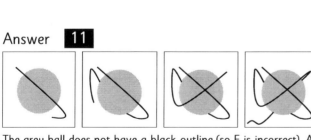

In each new cell any vertical grey threads, that have not yet crossed all 3 horizontal black threads, now move forward one step. Alternating junctions are over and under.

Answer 11

The grey ball does not have a black outline (so F is incorrect). A black string crosses it, its course lengthening with each new cell. Alternate crossings are in front of and behind the ball.

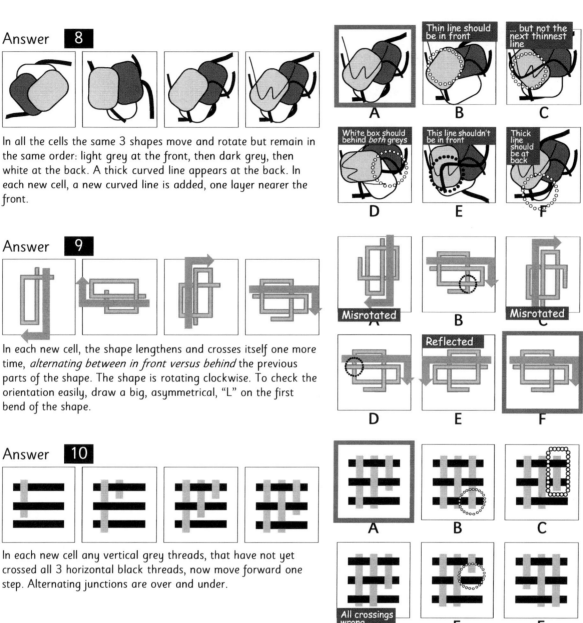

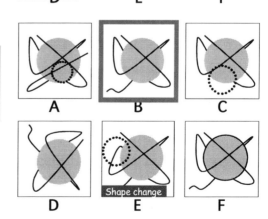

Answer 12

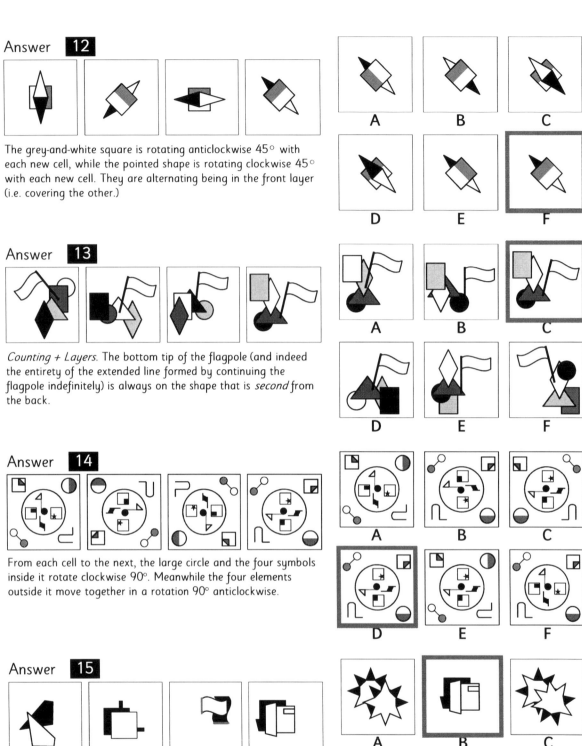

The grey-and-white square is rotating anticlockwise 45° with each new cell, while the pointed shape is rotating clockwise 45° with each new cell. They are alternating being in the front layer (i.e. covering the other.)

Answer 13

Counting + Layers. The bottom tip of the flagpole (and indeed the entirety of the extended line formed by continuing the flagpole indefinitely) is always on the shape that is *second* from the back.

Answer 14

From each cell to the next, the large circle and the four symbols inside it rotate clockwise 90°. Meanwhile the four elements outside it move together in a rotation 90° anticlockwise.

Answer 15

The shape in front reappears as a *entirely* black shape behind, rotated anticlockwise 90°.

This is the end of this session.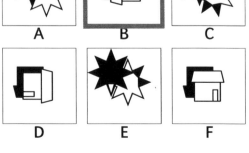

Training Session 4

As you rise through the Non-Verbal Ninja Training Course, you are gaining experience in detecting an ever wider range of rules.

This training session adds a new class of rules, but don't forget the rules you learned previously!

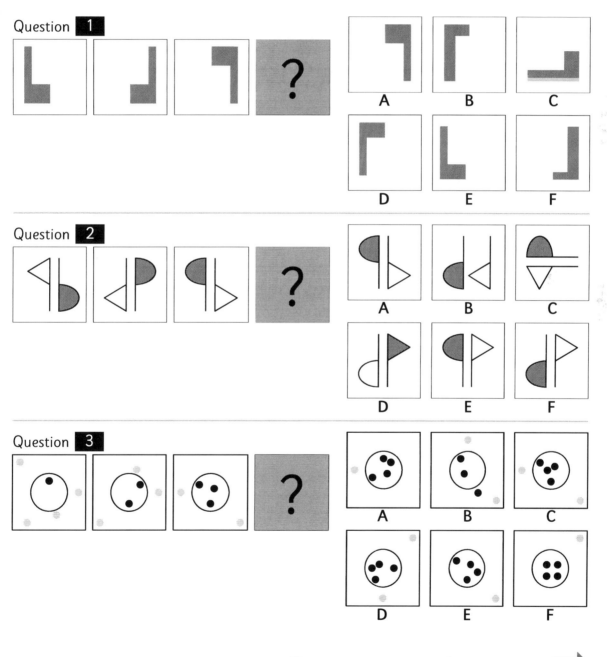

Question 1

Question 2

Question 3

Go to the next page

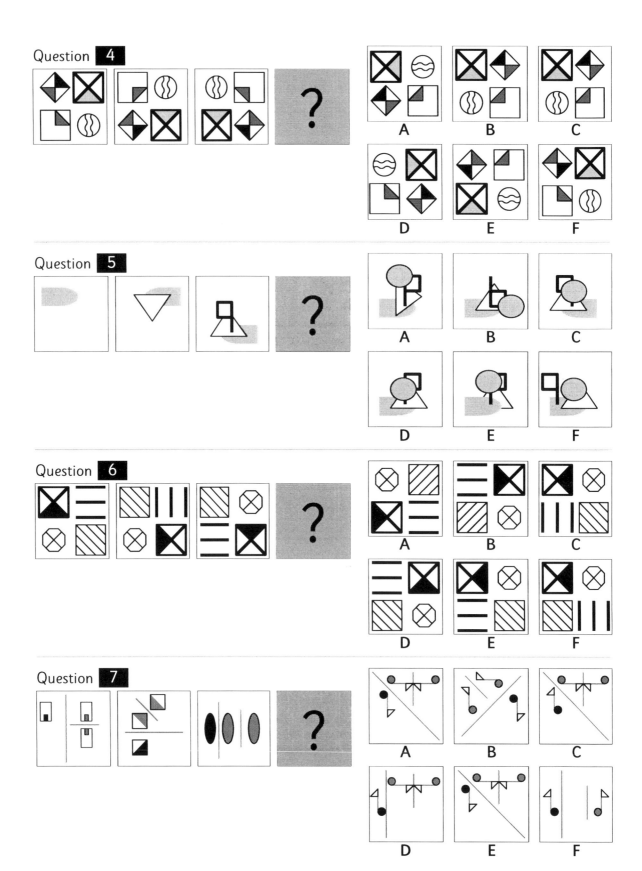

Question 4

Question 5

Question 6

Question 7

Go to the next page ➡

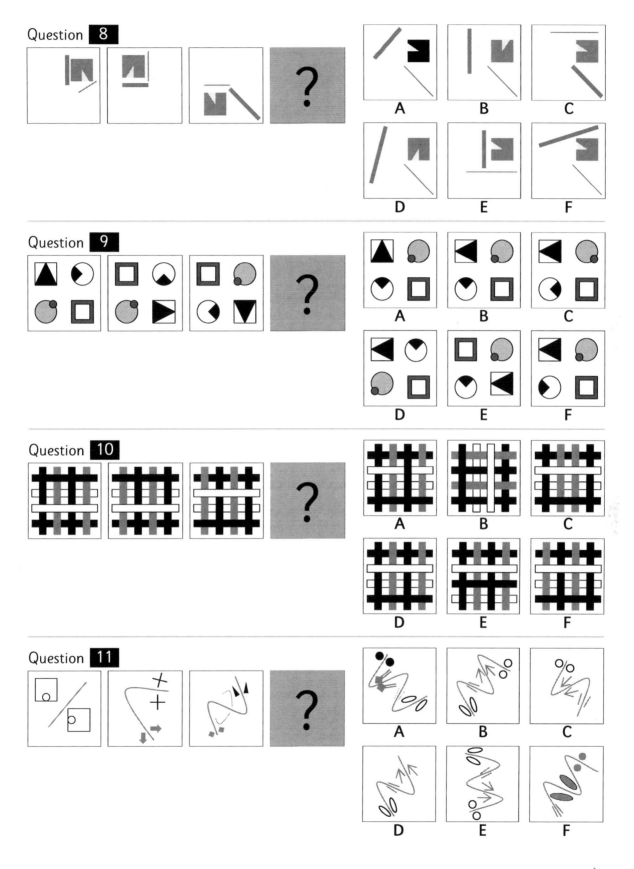

Question 8

Question 9

Question 10

Question 11

Go to the next page

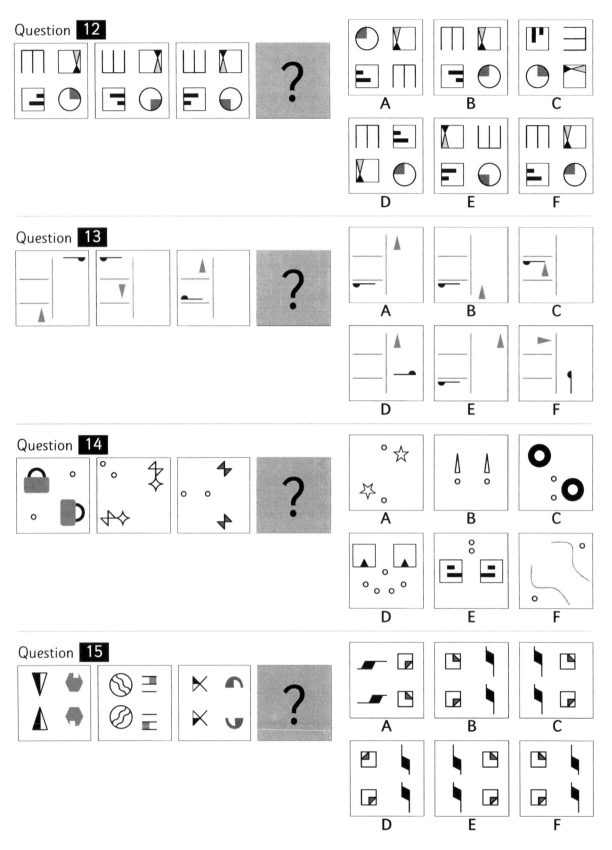

Question 12

Question 13

Question 14

Question 15

This is the end of this session.

Reflection

You have now learned the subtle distinction between reflection and rotation. No amount of rotation can make an object look like its reflection (unless the object has mirror symmetry).

Answer **1**

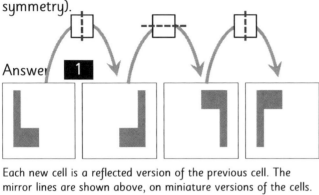

Each new cell is a reflected version of the previous cell. The mirror lines are shown above, on miniature versions of the cells.

Answer **2**

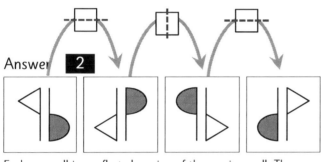

Each new cell is a reflected version of the previous cell. The mirror lines are shown above, on miniature versions of the cells. These slightly more complex cells require more checking to identify the correct answer.

Answer **3**

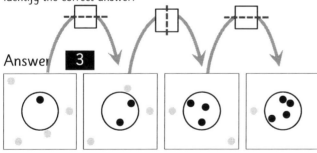

The same reflection process is occurring here, but at each stage one grey dot is removed from inside the circle and one black dot added outside.

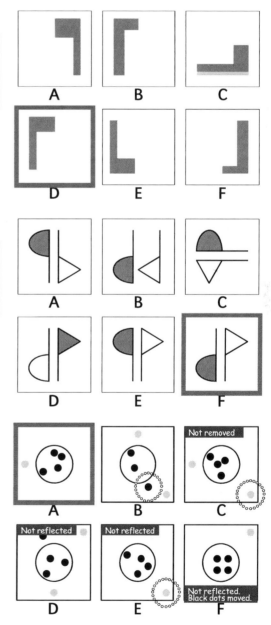

Go to the next page ➡

Answer 4

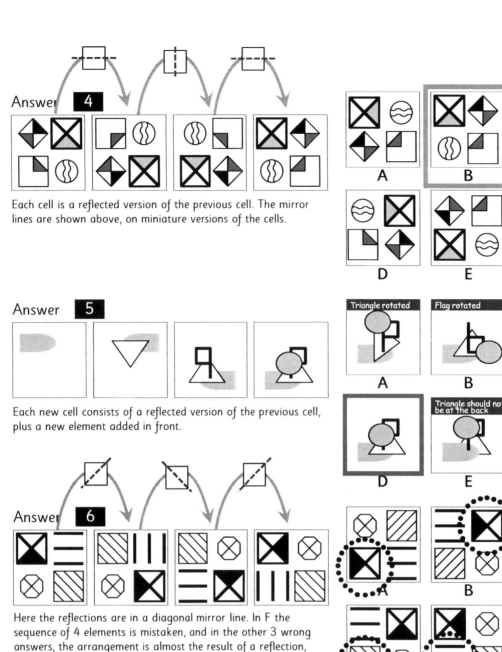

Each cell is a reflected version of the previous cell. The mirror lines are shown above, on miniature versions of the cells.

Answer 5

Each new cell consists of a reflected version of the previous cell, plus a new element added in front.

Answer 6

Here the reflections are in a diagonal mirror line. In F the sequence of 4 elements is mistaken, and in the other 3 wrong answers, the arrangement is almost the result of a reflection, except for one error, marked. Watch out for such asymmetrical elements.

Answer 7

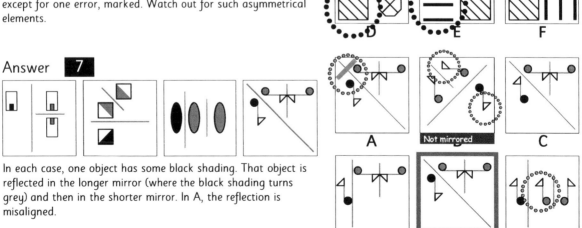

In each case, one object has some black shading. That object is reflected in the longer mirror (where the black shading turns grey) and then in the shorter mirror. In A, the reflection is misaligned.

Go to the next page ▶

Answer 8

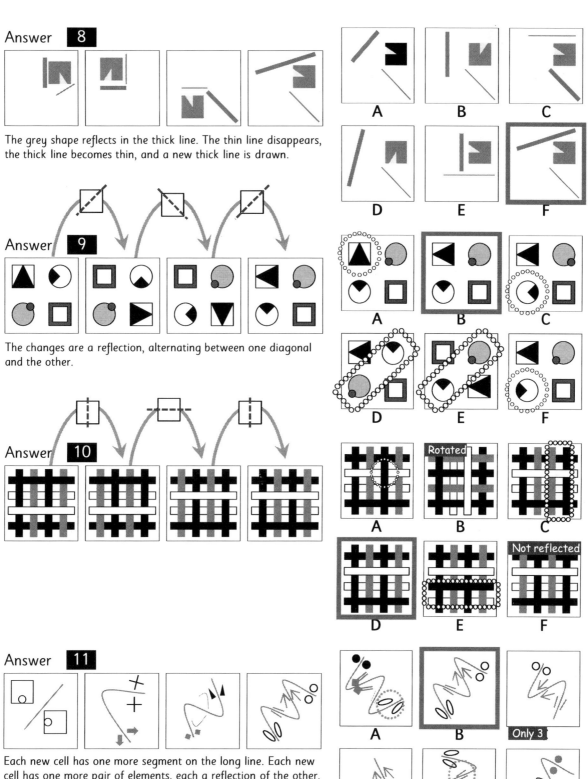

The grey shape reflects in the thick line. The thin line disappears, the thick line becomes thin, and a new thick line is drawn.

Answer 9

The changes are a reflection, alternating between one diagonal and the other.

Answer 10

Answer 11

Each new cell has one more segment on the long line. Each new cell has one more pair of elements, each a reflection of the other, with a local part of the long line being the line of reflection.

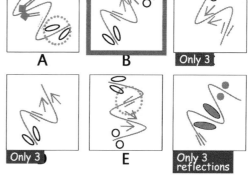

Go to the next page ➡

Answer 12

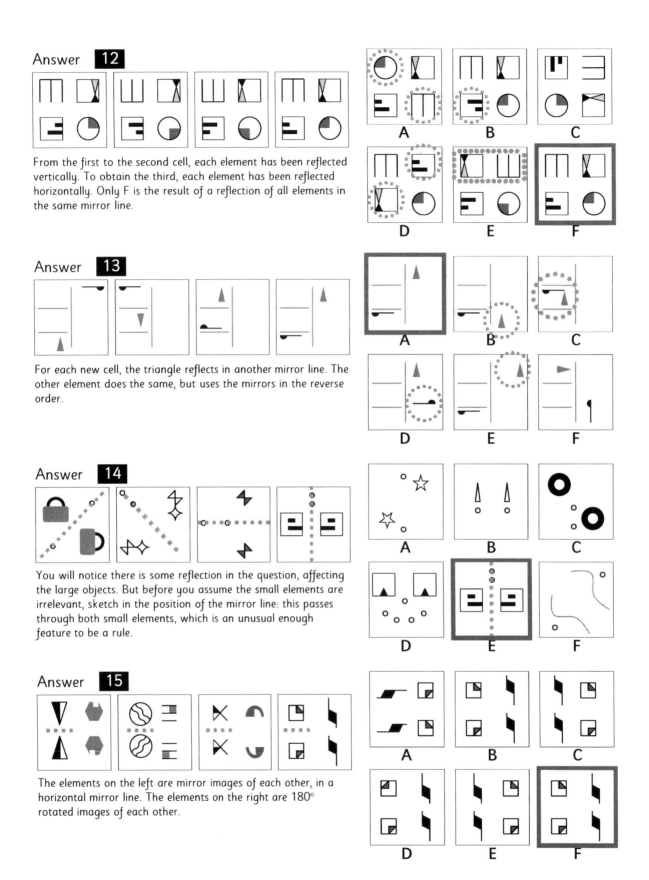

From the first to the second cell, each element has been reflected vertically. To obtain the third, each element has been reflected horizontally. Only F is the result of a reflection of all elements in the same mirror line.

Answer 13

For each new cell, the triangle reflects in another mirror line. The other element does the same, but uses the mirrors in the reverse order.

Answer 14

You will notice there is some reflection in the question, affecting the large objects. But before you assume the small elements are irrelevant, sketch in the position of the mirror line: this passes through both small elements, which is an unusual enough feature to be a rule.

Answer 15

The elements on the left are mirror images of each other, in a horizontal mirror line. The elements on the right are 180° rotated images of each other.

This is the end of this session.

Training Session 5

Well done, young ninja! You are making fine progress in the training course.

We now introduce another type of rule. You will quickly recognise what it is, but can you apply it consistently, together with all the previous rules, with total accuracy? That is the challenge.

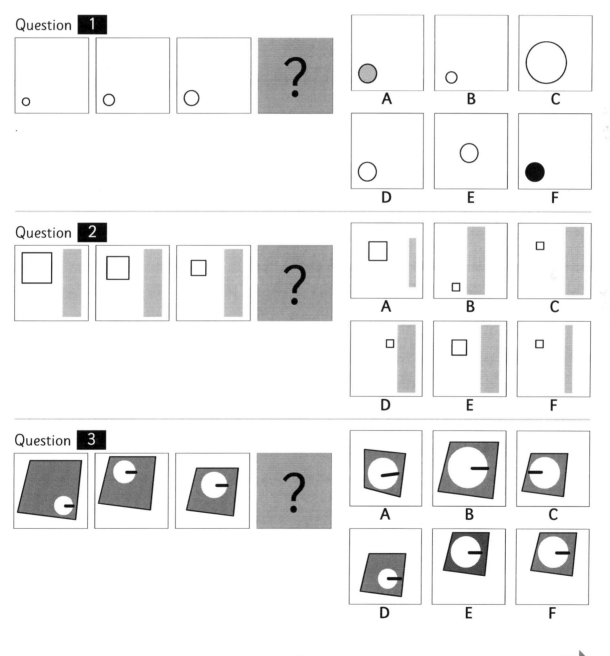

Go to the next page

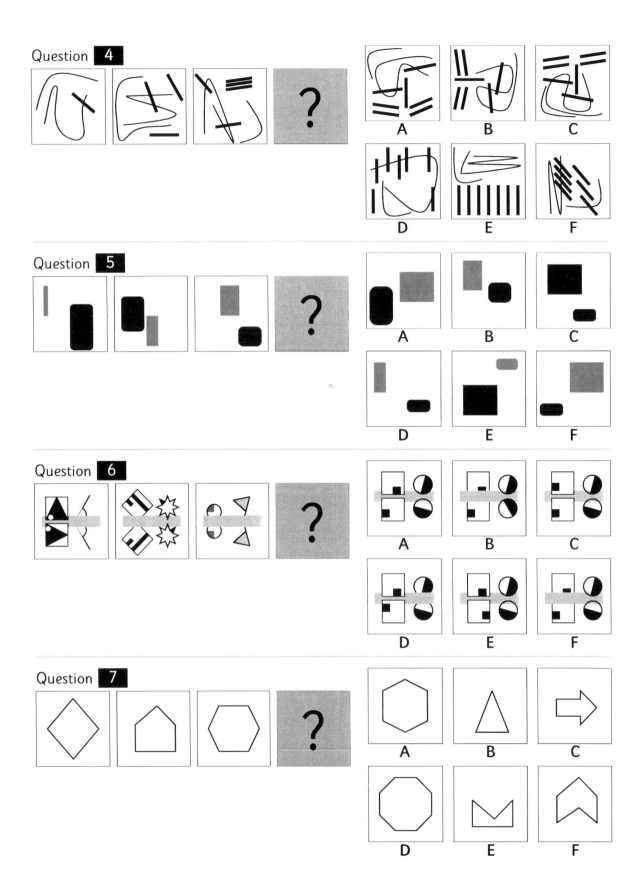

Question 4

Question 5

Question 6

Question 7

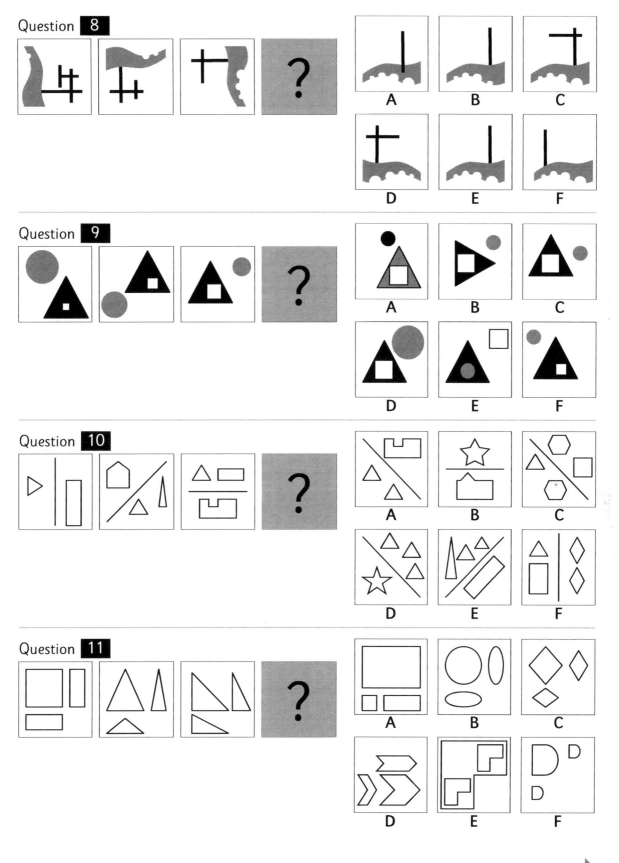

Question 8

Question 9

Question 10

Question 11

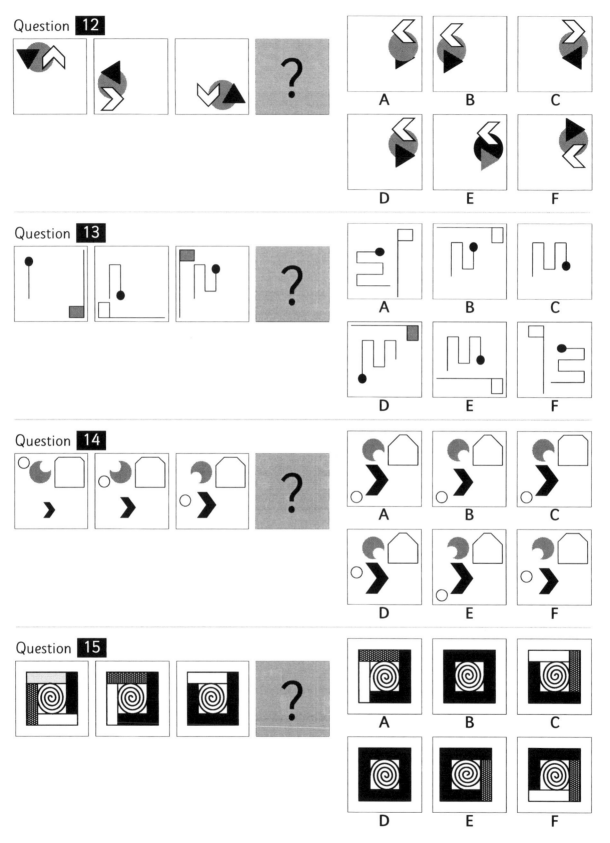

Question 12

Question 13

Question 14

Question 15

A   B   C

D   E   F

This is the end of this session.

Size

You have now learned about progressive growing and shrinking. This can be done evenly in both directions (so that squares remain squares, for example) or in just one direction (so that squares become rectangles) or to different extents in the two directions (again changing squares into rectangles).

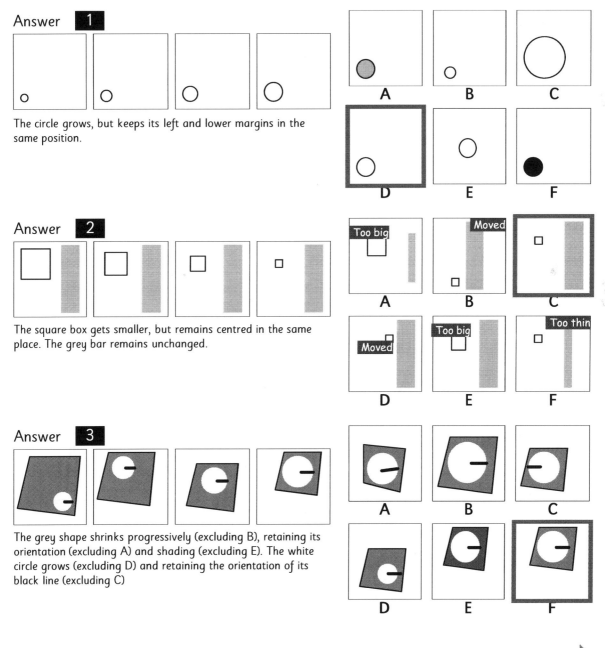

Answer 1

The circle grows, but keeps its left and lower margins in the same position.

Answer 2

The square box gets smaller, but remains centred in the same place. The grey bar remains unchanged.

Answer 3

The grey shape shrinks progressively (excluding B), retaining its orientation (excluding A) and shading (excluding E). The white circle grows (excluding D) and retaining the orientation of its black line (excluding C)

41

Go to the next page ➡

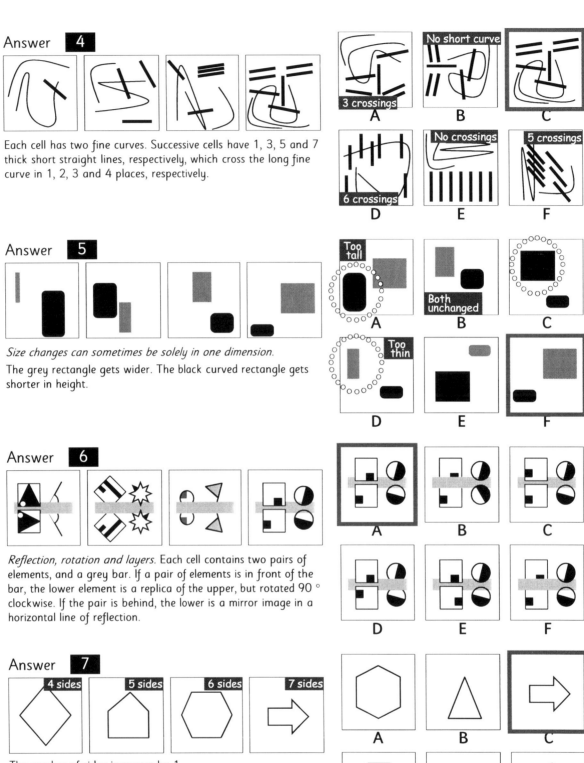

Answer 4

Each cell has two fine curves. Successive cells have 1, 3, 5 and 7 thick short straight lines, respectively, which cross the long fine curve in 1, 2, 3 and 4 places, respectively.

Answer 5

Size changes can sometimes be solely in one dimension.
The grey rectangle gets wider. The black curved rectangle gets shorter in height.

Answer 6

Reflection, rotation and layers. Each cell contains two pairs of elements, and a grey bar. If a pair of elements is in front of the bar, the lower element is a replica of the upper, but rotated 90 ° clockwise. If the pair is behind, the lower is a mirror image in a horizontal line of reflection.

Answer 7

The number of sides increases by 1.

Go to the next page

Answer 8

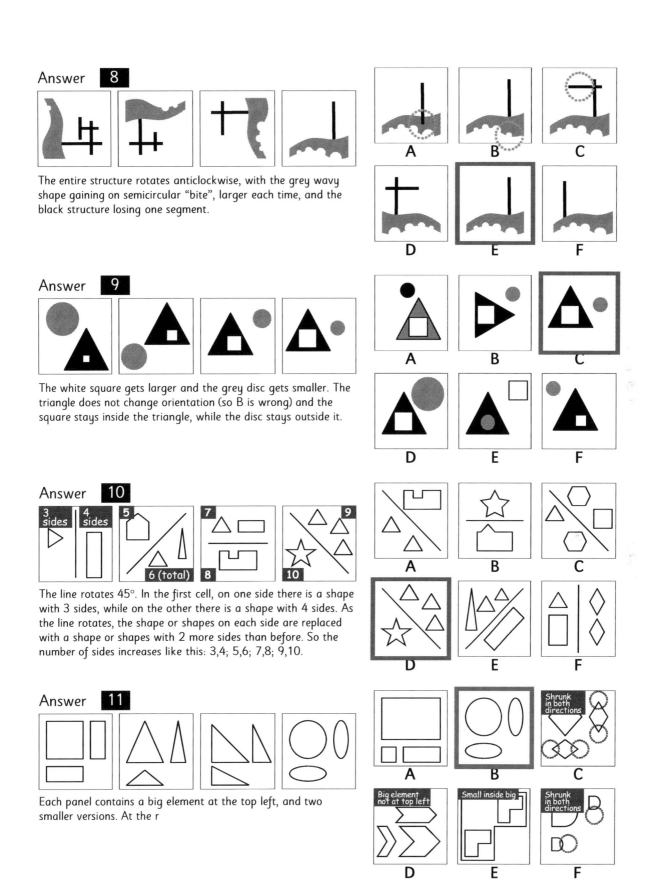

The entire structure rotates anticlockwise, with the grey wavy shape gaining on semicircular "bite", larger each time, and the black structure losing one segment.

Answer 9

The white square gets larger and the grey disc gets smaller. The triangle does not change orientation (so B is wrong) and the square stays inside the triangle, while the disc stays outside it.

Answer 10

The line rotates 45°. In the first cell, on one side there is a shape with 3 sides, while on the other there is a shape with 4 sides. As the line rotates, the shape or shapes on each side are replaced with a shape or shapes with 2 more sides than before. So the number of sides increases like this: 3,4; 5,6; 7,8; 9,10.

Answer 11

Each panel contains a big element at the top left, and two smaller versions. At the r

43

Go to the next page ▶

Answer

The structure moves anticlockwise around the cell, but rotates around its own centre clockwise. The grey circle remains at the back.

A   B   C

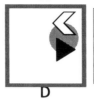 

D   E   F

Answer 13

 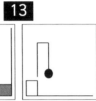

The flag element moves around the cell clockwise, alternating between white and shaded. The other element is a line which gains two segments at each stage, with the black disc moving to the outer end of the newly created segments.

A   B   C

D   E   F

Answer 14

  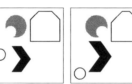

1. The circle moves progressively down.
2. The crescent shape rotates anticlockwise 90°.
3. The rectangle has progressively larger bites in its top corners.
4. The chevron grows progressively.

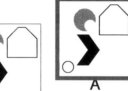 

A   Not grown   Bites are too small

Too high   Rotated   All wrong

Answer 15

The inner spiral stays stationary. The outer four rectangles rotate as a group clockwise, but then the rectangle on the right is made black, so that gradually all the rectangles become black.

  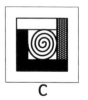

A   B   C

D   E   F

This is the end of this session.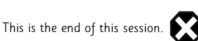

Training Session 6

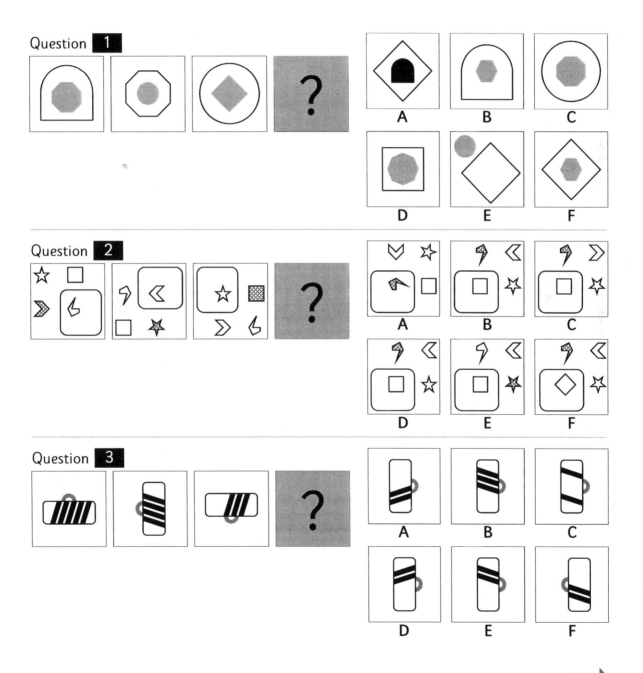

Question **1**

Question **2**

Question **3**

Go to the next page ➡

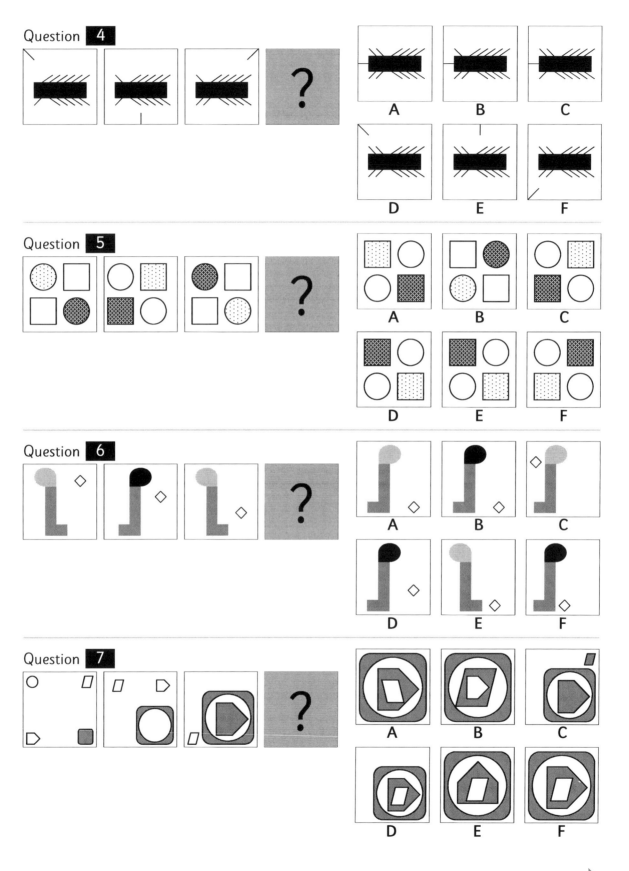

Question 4

Question 5

Question 6

Question 7

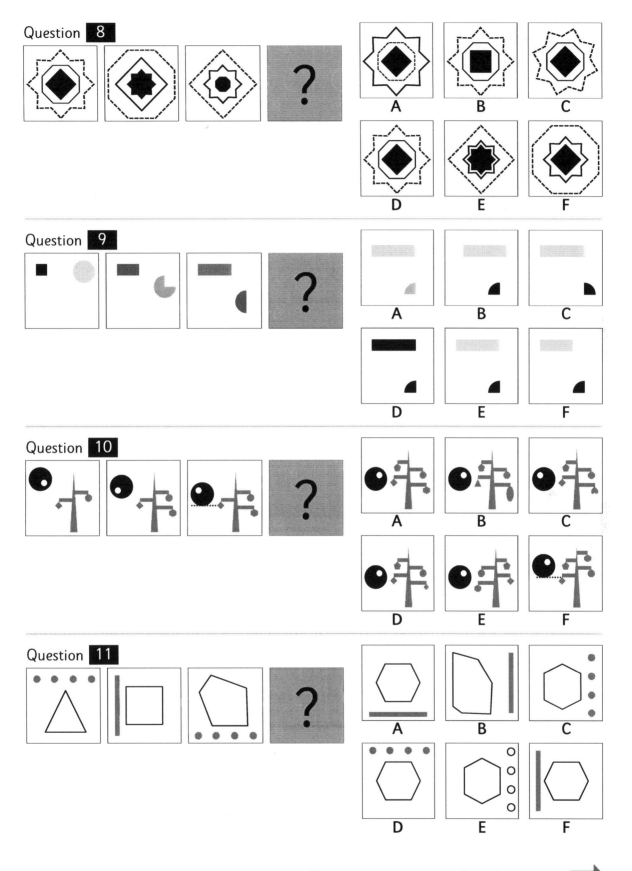

Question 8

Question 9

Question 10

Question 11

Go to the next page

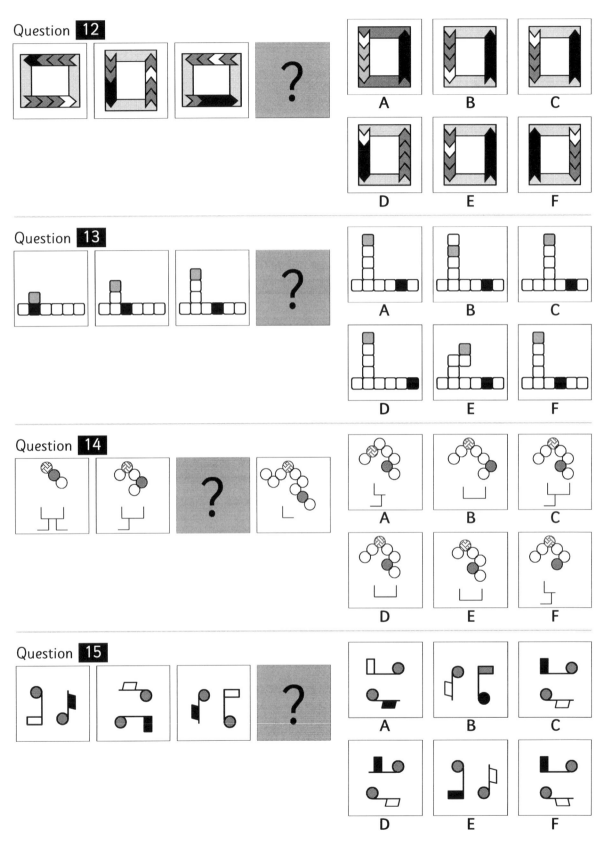

Question 12

Question 13

Question 14

Question 15

This is the end of this session.

Answers to Session 6

You are now learning to solve puzzles using multiple rules, including a new rule, **inside versus outside**. Make sure you understand all the explanations, especially in cases where you had difficulty.

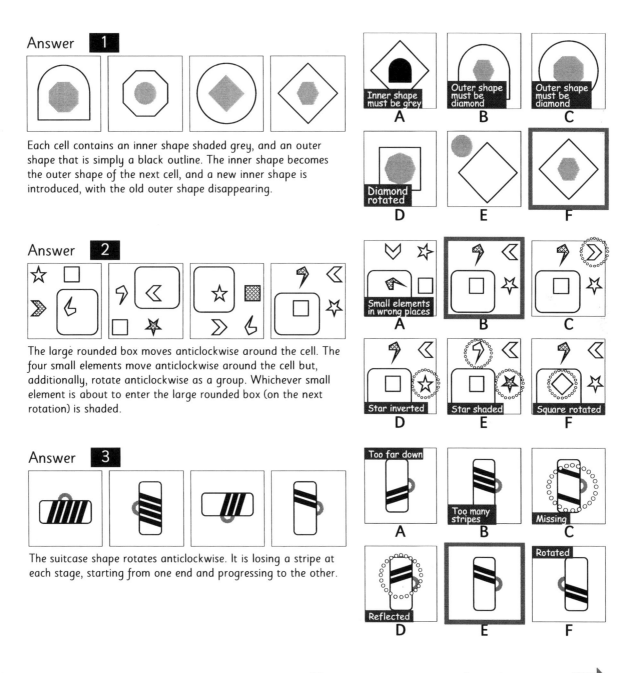

Answer 1

Each cell contains an inner shape shaded grey, and an outer shape that is simply a black outline. The inner shape becomes the outer shape of the next cell, and a new inner shape is introduced, with the old outer shape disappearing.

Answer 2

The large rounded box moves anticlockwise around the cell. The four small elements move anticlockwise around the cell but, additionally, rotate anticlockwise as a group. Whichever small element is about to enter the large rounded box (on the next rotation) is shaded.

Answer 3

The suitcase shape rotates anticlockwise. It is losing a stripe at each stage, starting from one end and progressing to the other.

Go to the next page ➡

Answer 4

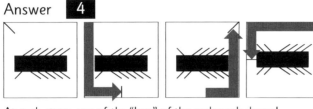

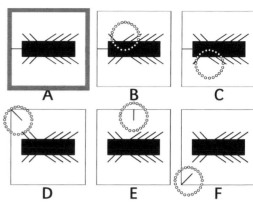

At each stage, one of the "legs" of the cockroach-shaped structure flips left. The outer line moves anticlockwise around the design, by 3/8 of a circle. **Tip**: This is more than ¼, and less than ½ (which would send the outer line diagonally opposite) and so the line alternates between diagonal and straight horizontal/vertical.

Answer 5

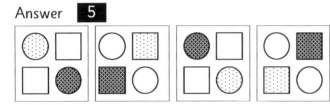

The elements stay in the same position but the pattern of shading rotates clockwise 90°. This is easy to see below with four identical shapes to eliminate the distraction of shapes.

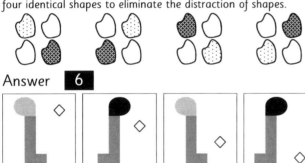

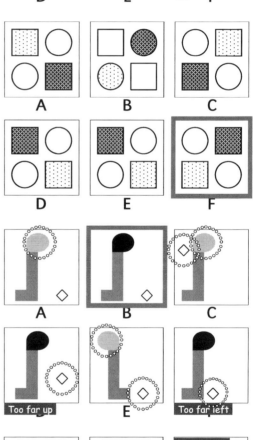

Answer 6

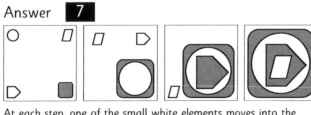

The main element mirrors in a vertical line, with its top part alternating between black and light grey.

A small diamond is falling from top to bottom, on the right.

Answer 7

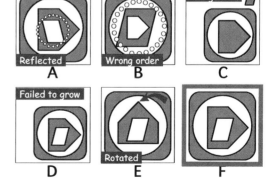

At each step, one of the small white elements moves into the grey rounded box, as a new inner element: these new inner elements alternate in colour between white and grey. The grey rounded box and its contents grow. Several options fit this rule so you must look for another rule that is less obvious: no elements rotate.

Go to the next page ⬤

Answer 8

Each cell has 3 elements: inner, middle and outer. At each step, the inner and middle element move outwards by one position, and the outer becomes the inner. Whichever is inner is shaded black. Whichever is outer has a dashed outline.

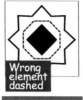 

Answer 9

The square gradually extends horizontally and becomes paler. The disc moves down, becomes darker, and loses ¼ of a disc of area (the location of the "bite" moving clockwise).

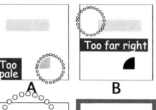

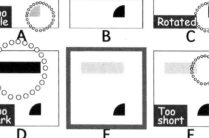

Answer 10

The black disc moves down steadily. It is spinning clockwise 90° per step. The tree-like structure gains another branch and a small element dangling from it. You can see from the 2nd and 3rd cells that the new branches do not appear in order of position.

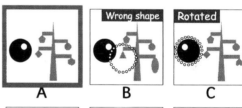

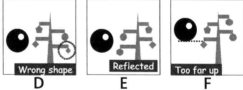

Answer 11

The central element gains one side. It is not necessary for it to have equal sides or angles, as proven by the third cell. The outer element rotates anticlockwise around the cell, and alternates between 4 grey discs and a single grey bar.

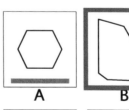

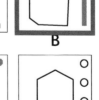 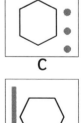

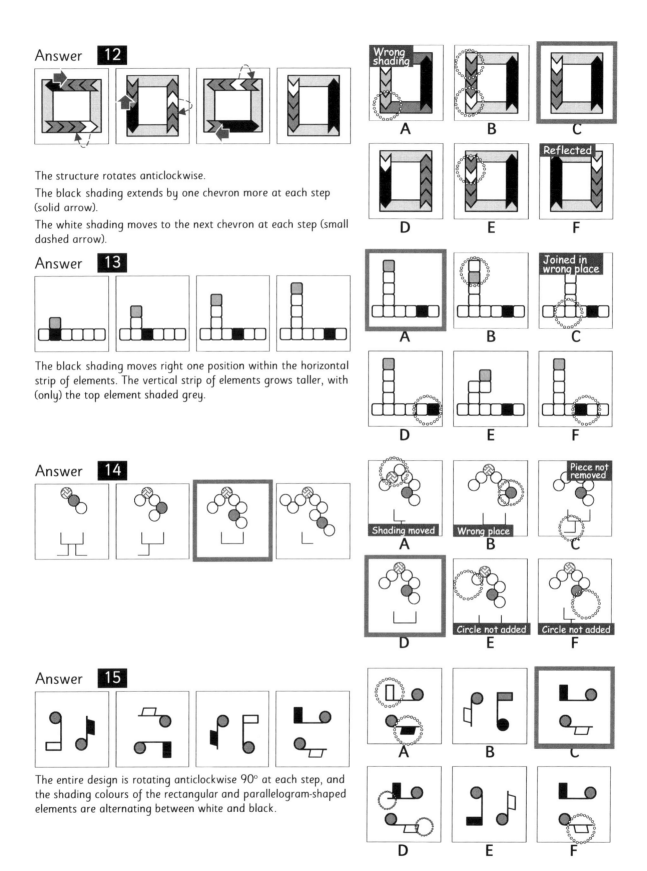

Answer 12

The structure rotates anticlockwise.

The black shading extends by one chevron more at each step (solid arrow).

The white shading moves to the next chevron at each step (small dashed arrow).

Answer 13

The black shading moves right one position within the horizontal strip of elements. The vertical strip of elements grows taller, with (only) the top element shaded grey.

Answer 14

Answer 15

The entire design is rotating anticlockwise 90° at each step, and the shading colours of the rectangular and parallelogram-shaped elements are alternating between white and black.

This is the end of this session. ✖

Training Session 7

Advanced Ninja Training

Now that you can do the simple type of puzzle, with one unknown cell amongst four, it is time to move to the more complex design, where there are 2 missing out of 6. The additional ninja skill you have to gain is rejecting "dead ends". These are choices for the first unknown that seem fine on their own, but would leave you with no suitable choices for the *second* unknown.

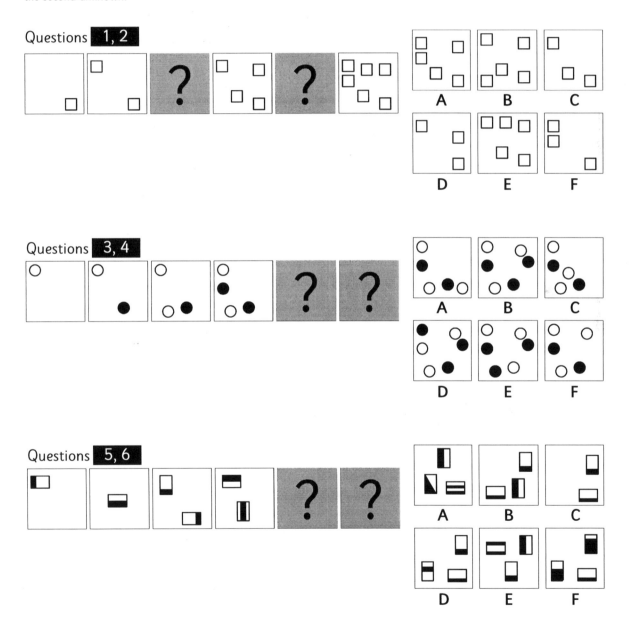

Questions **1, 2**

Questions **3, 4**

Questions **5, 6**

Go to the next page ➡

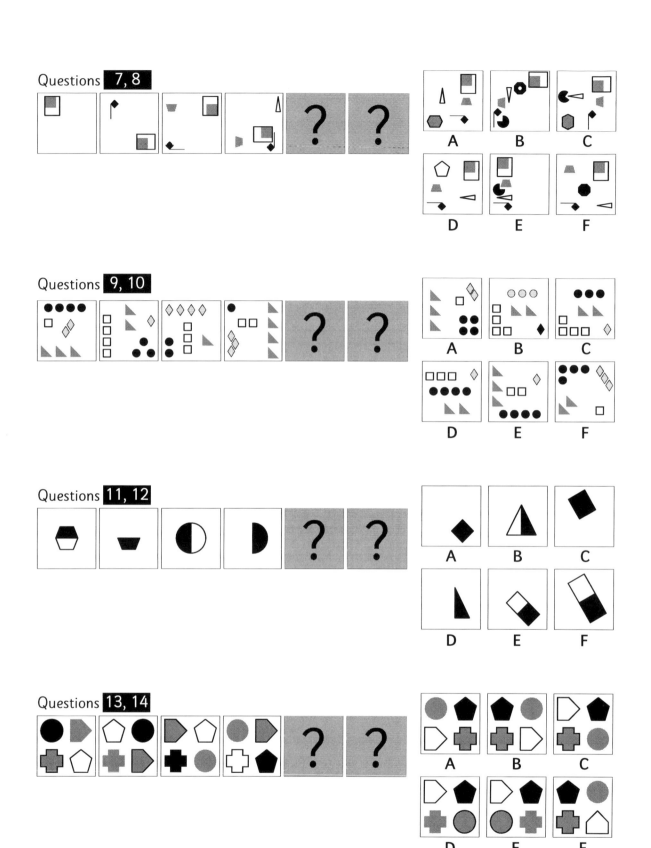

Go to the next page

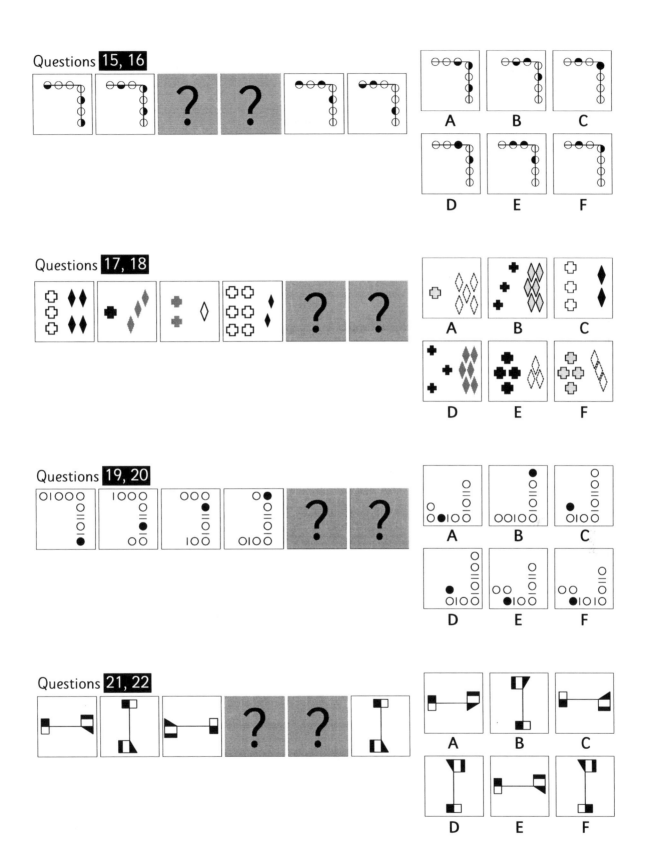

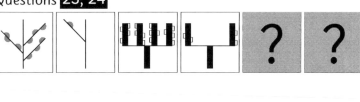

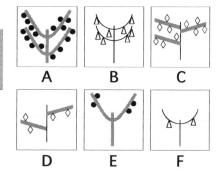

A   B   C

D   E   F

Questions 25, 26

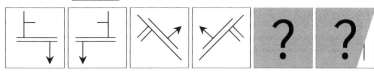

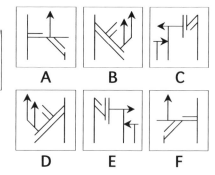

A   B   C

D   E   F

Questions 27, 28

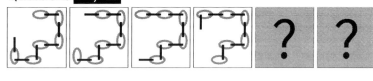

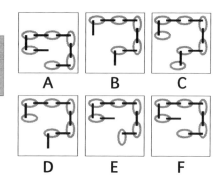

A   B   C

D   E   F

Questions 29, 30

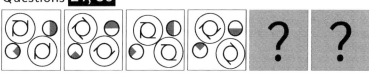

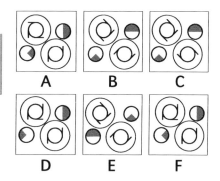

A   B   C

D   E   F

56

Go to the next page

Answers to Session 7

Congratulations! You are now on the top level of ninja training, solving two mysteries per sequence.

Make sure you understand the concept of a "dead end" option for the first uknown. Such an option seams to fit a pattern, but makes it impossible to solve the second unknown. This challenge only occurs in puzzles with 2 unknown cells, and not in the simple junior ninja puzzles with 1 unknown cell.

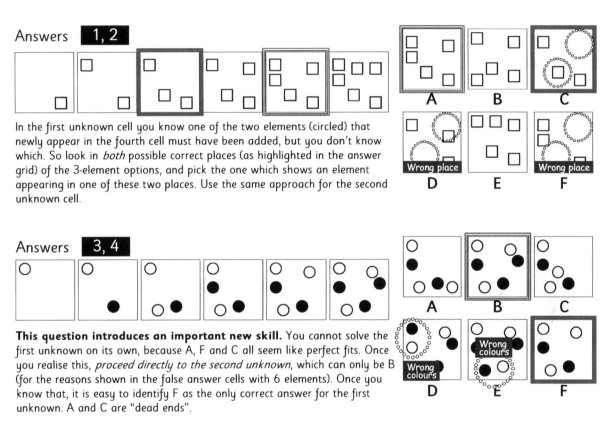

Answers 1, 2

In the first unknown cell you know one of the two elements (circled) that newly appear in the fourth cell must have been added, but you don't know which. So look in *both* possible correct places (as highlighted in the answer grid) of the 3-element options, and pick the one which shows an element appearing in one of these two places. Use the same approach for the second unknown cell.

Answers 3, 4

This question introduces an important new skill. You cannot solve the first unknown on its own, because A, F and C all seem like perfect fits. Once you realise this, *proceed directly to the second unknown*, which can only be B (for the reasons shown in the false answer cells with 6 elements). Once you know that, it is easy to identify F as the only correct answer for the first unknown. A and C are "dead ends".

Answers 5, 6

The elements alternate between quarter shaded black and half shaded black. The number of elements increases by one, every second step. You may not have expected a diagonal division of the element, but this is the only division that gives the right proportions.

Go to the next page ➡

Answers

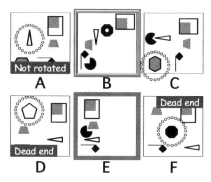

In each cell, a new element appears. The elements of the previous cell appear again, but rotated 90 degrees anticlockwise and in a different position. Two options, which at first seem possible for the first unknown cell, are "dead ends", because if they are chosen there is no suitable option for the second unknown cell.

Answers 9, 10

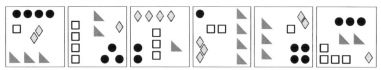

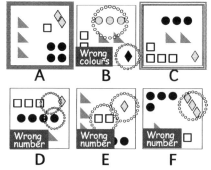

In each cell, there are 1, 2, 3 and 4 instances of each of four shapes, respectively. The counts rotate: the shape that had 4 instances becomes 3, the shape that had 3 becomes 2, 2 becomes 1 and 1 becomes 4.

Answers 11, 12

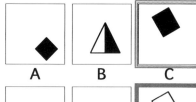

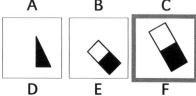

In each pair of cells, in the move from the left cell of the pair to the right cell, the black half disappears and the white half remains, becoming black. In the wrong answers, it is the white half that disappears.

Answers 13, 14

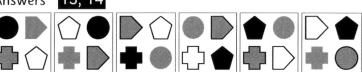

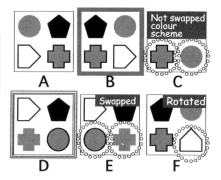

Two things are happening simultaneously. Three elements (not the cross) are moving positions in a clockwise cycle. However, whichever element arrives in the bottom right position then swaps colour schemes with the cross.

Go to the next page

Answers 15, 16

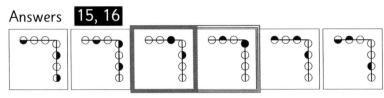

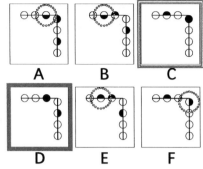

The dark shading travels anticlockwise on the outer part of the shape and clockwise on the inner part of the shape, swapping from inner to outer at the end of the line. The correct answers happen to each have complete shaded discs, which are not seen in any of the visible cells in the question. This question considers each half-disc as independent.

Answers 17, 18

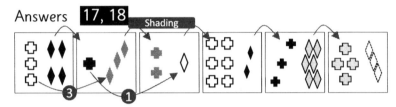

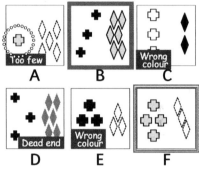

On the left there is always a number of crosses. On the right there is always a number of diamonds. In each successive cell, the **number** of diamonds always equals the number of crosses in the previous cell, and a new number of crosses is created. Meanwhile, the **shading scheme** of the crosses matches the shading scheme of the diamonds in the previous cell, and the diamonds gain a new shading scheme.

Answers 19, 20

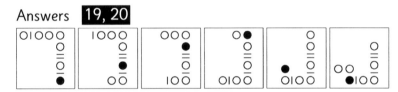

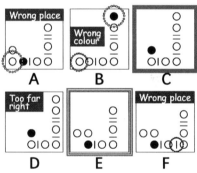

There is a snake-shaped trail of elements. At each step, one element is removed from one end and added to the other end. Black shading is moving in the opposite direction, but in the discs only. You have to guess what happens when this shading reaches the end of the trail. It travels with the element that moves to the other end of the trail.

Answers 21, 22

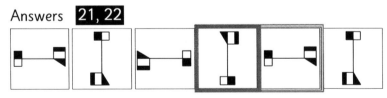

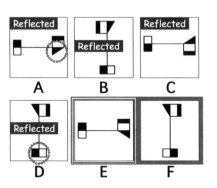

This is not simply a 90 degree clockwise rotation. The shape is also being reflected, with the mirror line being its long central spindle.

Go to the next page

Answers 23, 24

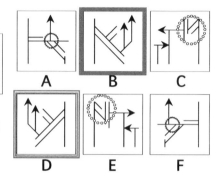

In each pair, there is a certain design of main stalk, of branches, and of small elements attached to branches. In every cell, the number of small elements attached to each branch equals the number of branches. We do not know what designs of stalk, branches and small elements are present in the unknown cells. We just need to find the design for which two cells fit the pattern: A and E. Which comes first? The clue is that in the first and second pairs shown, more branches come before fewer branches.

Answers  25, 26

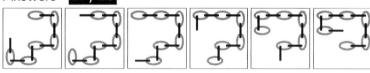

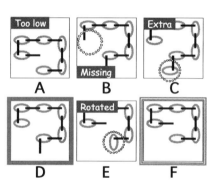

Each pair is a reflection in a vertical mirror line. There is only one pair of correct mirror images amongst the options. The small amount of the second unknown shape that is revealed allows determination of which is the first unknown and which the second.

Answers 27, 28

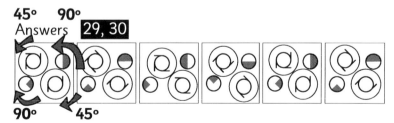

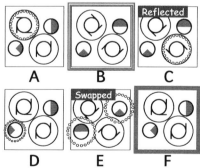

The shape consists of a chain.
At each step, one element is removed from the one end and added to the other end.

45° 90°
Answers 29, 30

90° 45°

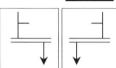

The discs are turning, in the directions and with the speeds per step shown.

Go to the next page

Training Session 8

Gain speed, accuracy and confidence on this upper plateau of Ninja skill. Here are some more of the tougher "2-unknown-in-6" puzzles of the Sequence type.

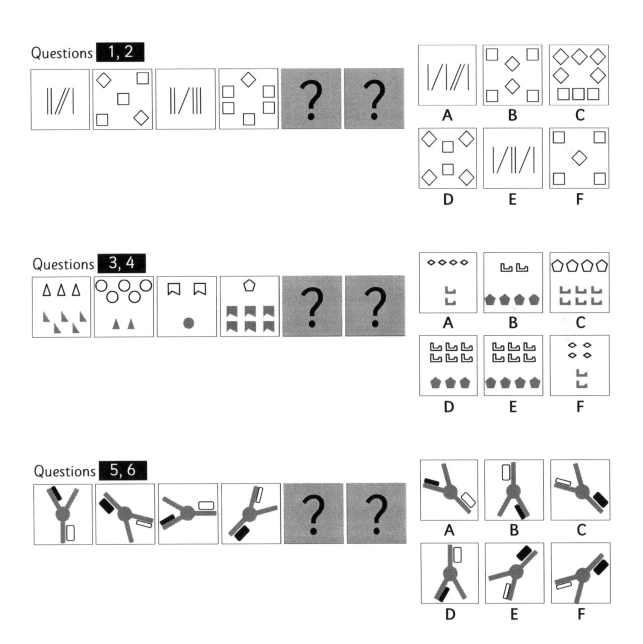

Go to the next page

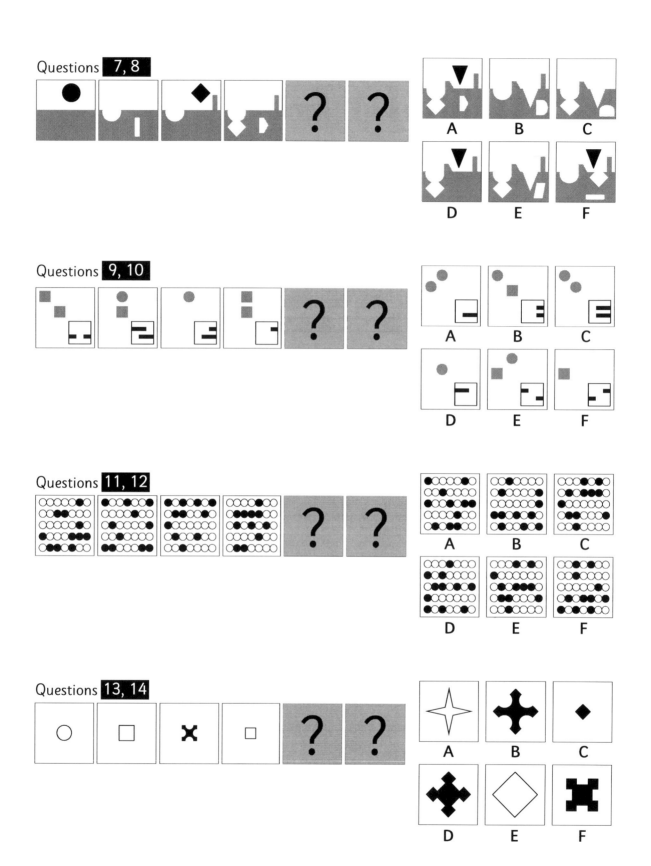

Questions **7, 8**

Questions **9, 10**

Questions **11, 12**

Questions **13, 14**

62

Go to the next page

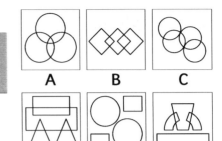

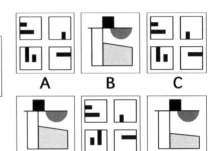

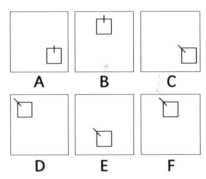

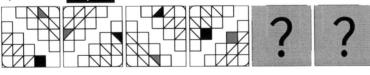

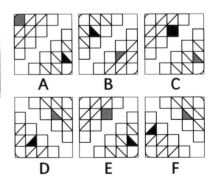

Go to the next page

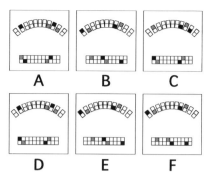

Questions 25, 26

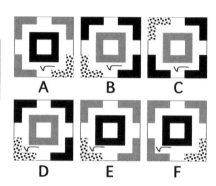

Questions 27, 28

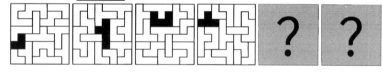

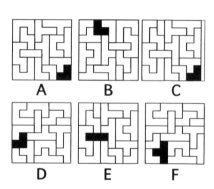

Questions 29, 30

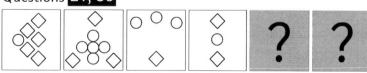

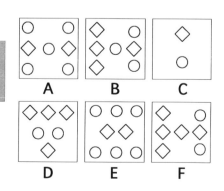

Go to the next page

You may have found quite a few of these questions challenging, young ninja, because they are designed to keep stretching the boundaries of your experience, and broaden the range of rules you look for.

Answers 1, 2

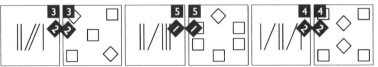

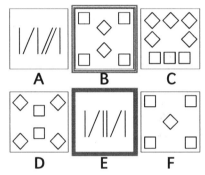

In each pair of cells, the number of vertical lines in the left cell equals the number of squares (aligned straight) in the right cell, and the number of oblique lines in the left cell equals the number of diamonds (or obliquely oriented squares) in the right cell.

Answers 3, 4

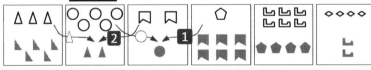

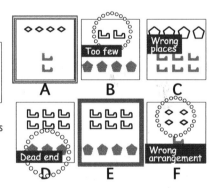

The elements in the top half are always outlined in black with no shading; those in the bottom row are always shaded grey with no outline. The shapes move downward and to the right, while the counts (and grid arrangements) of the elements move downward and to the left.

Answers 5, 6

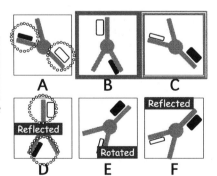

The shape is rotating by a 90 + 45 = 135 degrees. You can tell this because the stalk that is downwards at first moves in the next step to the top left corner. At the next step it is pointing directly sideways, and so on. Meanwhile, the colours of the blocks are alternating.

65

Go to the next page

Answers

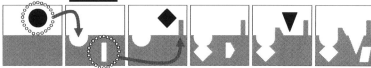

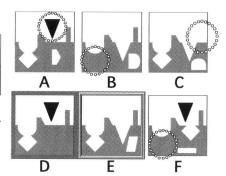

The upper half is white and the lower half grey.

In the first cell (and all odd cells) a black element is shown once in the upper half. In all later cells, part of this shape is used to extend the white half into the grey half (or, to "bite" out of the grey half).

In the second cell (and all even cells) a white element is shown once in the lower half. In all later cells, part of this shape is used to extend the grey half into the white half.

Answers

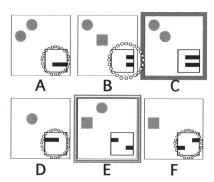

In the bottom right region there is an element containing small or large black blocks or both. In the top left there are grey squares or discs. Every small block is linked to a disc in the cell to the left; every large block is linked to a square in the cell to the left. The left/right alignments of the black blocks control the left/right positions of the grey elements.

Answers

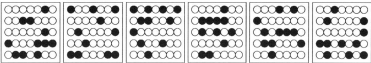

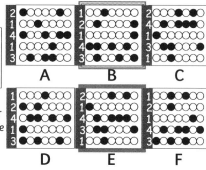

In the first cell, the numbers of black discs are, in the respective rows, 1,2,1,4,3. In successive cells, this pattern shifts downwards (with the number in the last row moving to the first row). The examiners have given you a clue by making the discs touch side-to-side but not top-to-bottom.

Answers

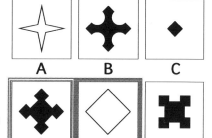

There are two sets of three cells. The element in the second cell appears in the third, shaded black, with four copies of half the element in the first cell bitten out of it. From the first 3 cells it is not obvious that the element in the first cell is rotated 45° before being used to bite out of the element in the third cell, but examining the options that is the only way a square can produce the required bites.

Go to the next page ▶

Answers 15, 16

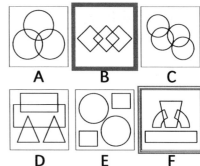

What is increasing steadily is not the number of shapes, but the number of regions, where an overlap between two shapes is counted as a region. The diagram above shows the counts of shapes and of the additional overlap regions, showing the total count rising progressively from 1 to 6.

Answers 17, 18

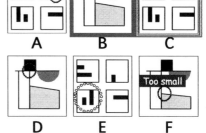

In each pair of cells the left and right cells are mirror images of each other in a vertical mirror line.

Answers 19, 20

    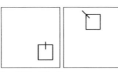

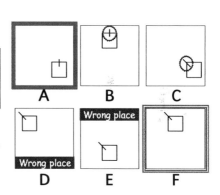

The square is moving anticlockwise around the cell by 90+45 degrees per step (illustrated by the dashed lines and small square and triangle). Meanwhile the short line is moving anticlockwise in angle by 45 degrees per step.

Answers 21, 22

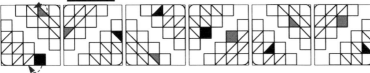

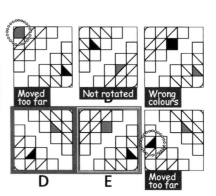

At each step the design rotates anticlockwise 90°.

One segment is shaded black and one is shaded grey. At each step the shading moves to another element that is adjacent (i.e. sharing a side). The first movement of each is shown by arrows.

Go to the next page ➡

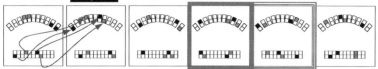

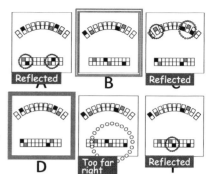

The lower pattern in each cell sets the upper pattern of the next cell, as shown by the arrows.

There is no particular rule for what appears in the lower pattern of each new cell, so do not waste time trying to find one. Instead, with the main rule you can exclude many answers and leave yourself with only the correct one.

To minimise risk of error, work forwards from the 3rd cell to answer the 4th cell, and work backwards from the 6th cell to answer the 5th cell.

Answers **25, 26**

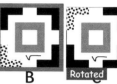

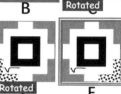

Three things are happening.

1. The overall design (as defined by the position of the speckled corner piece) is rotating anticlockwise 90° per step.
2. The inner square and three corner segments are alternating between black and grey.
3. The small curve is moving slowly clockwise in the gap between the inner square and outer corners, taking two steps to travel 90°.

Answers **27, 28**

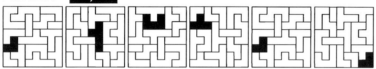

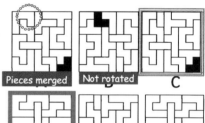

At each step the design rotates anticlockwise 90°. The design resembles a jigsaw, consisting of interlocking pieces. At each step, the shading moves to an adjacent element.

Answers **29, 30**

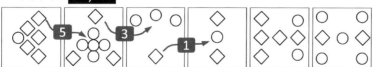

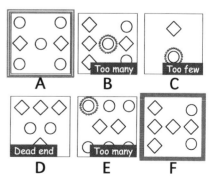

The number of diamonds in each cell determines the number of circles in the next cell. Although both D and F would fit the pattern for the first unknown cell, D is a dead end, because choosing it would leave no solution for the second unknown cell.

Go to the next page

Training Session 9

Armed with a broad range of ninja skills, tackle these more difficult sequence questions. Each will reinforce a rule you have already studied, or take you through the process of learning a new one.

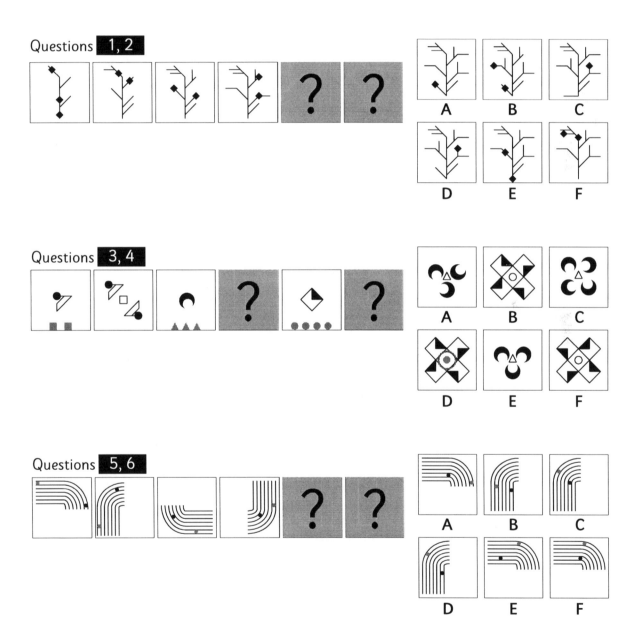

Go to the next page ➡

Questions **7, 8**

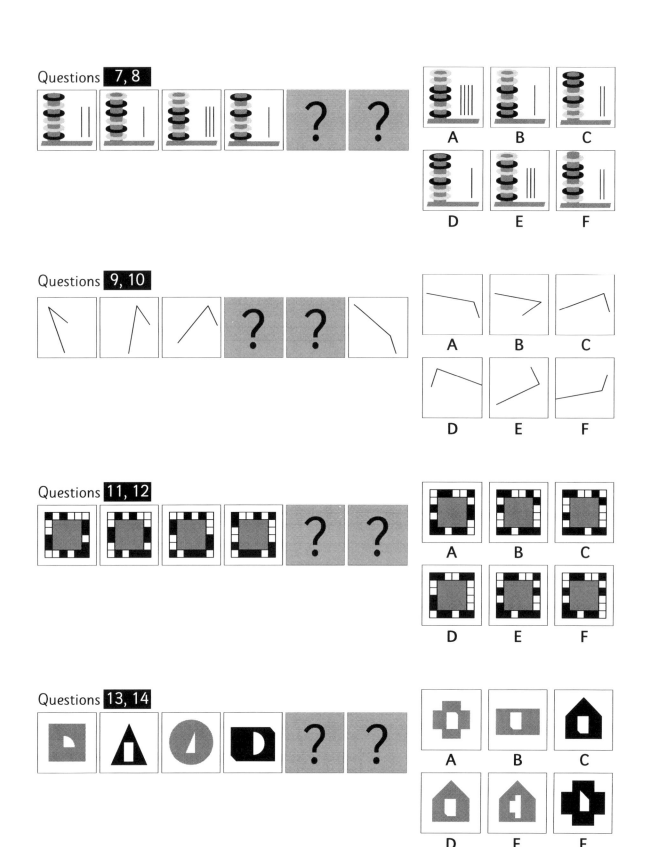

Questions **9, 10**

Questions **11, 12**

Questions **13, 14**

Go to the next page

Questions 15, 16

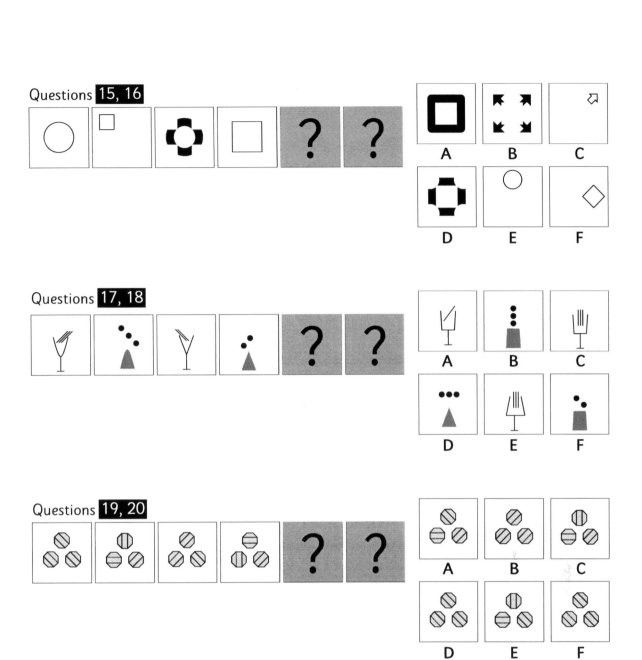

Questions 17, 18

Questions 19, 20

Questions 21, 22

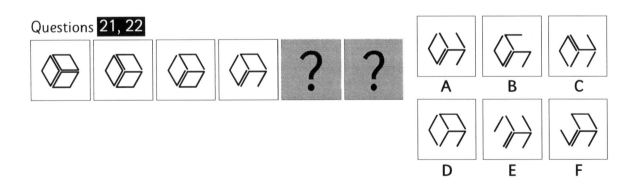

Go to the next page ▶

Questions 23, 24

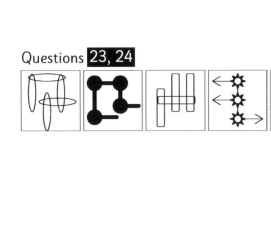

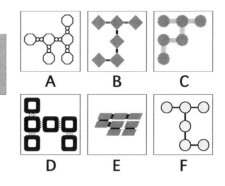

Questions 25, 26

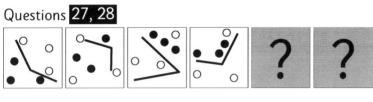

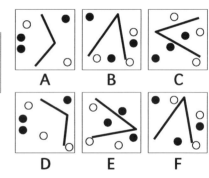

Questions 27, 28

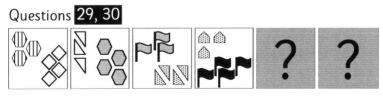

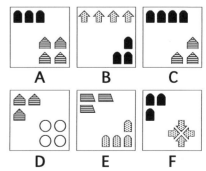

Questions 29, 30

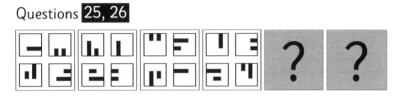

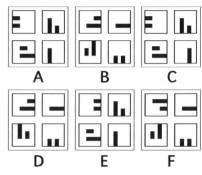

Go to the next page

Learn from all the questions you found challenging, by reflecting upon the explanations provided below.

Answers  1, 2

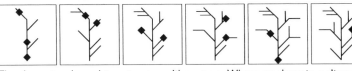

The shape is a branching structure, like a tree. Wherever there is a diamond, in the next cell a branch appears, at 45 degrees to the existing line at the point of the diamond. New diamonds appear without any particular pattern in their number or position.

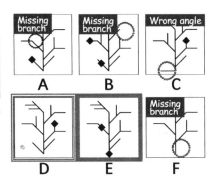

Answers 3, 4

In each pair, the number of grey elements at the bottom of the left cell tells you how many times the middle element will appear in the right cell. Each copy is rotated by an equal amount so that the total rotation is 360°. Meanwhile a single copy of the grey element appears in the centre of the right cell, drawn in black with no shading.

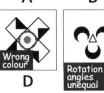

Answers 5, 6

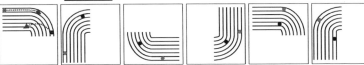

The entire design rotates anticlockwise. The grey disc moves along its track, as shown by the dotted line in this answer section. The black disc moves in the opposite direction but additionally jumps one track at each step, following the path shown here by its dotted line.

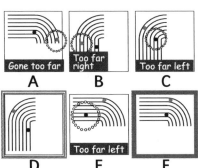 

Go to the next page ➡

 Answers **7,8**

At each step, the rings move downward by a certain number of steps. This number is given the number of vertical sticks on the right of the cell. The rings that reach the bottom disappear and reappear at the top. D is a dead end because it fits the rule for the first unknown but then leaves no options for the second unknown.

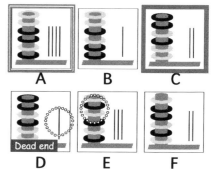

Answers **9,10**

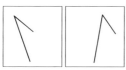 

The long part of the shape rotates clockwise. The angle of rotation is 30 degrees, which can be seen from the first and the third shapes having their long parts at right angles. The small part is attached at an angle: this angle progressively widens.

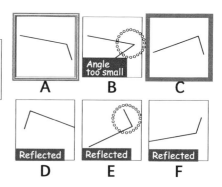

Answers **11,12**

The small black or white squares move clockwise around the big grey square. The easiest way to solve this is to count the groups of squares of each colour in the first cell, and then check that the same pattern (starting from the appropriate position) still holds on all later squares. Here the sequence is (clockwise from the top left) 1 black, 1 white, 1 black, 3 white ... or (more concisely) 1 1 1 3 2 1 3 1 1 2 2 2. Written like this, it is easy to check the various options.

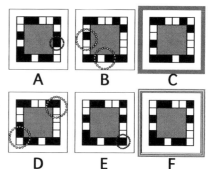

Answers **13,14**

The outer shape alternates between being filled in grey and being filled in black. Inside, a white inner shape is cut out, which is exactly half (by cutting vertically) the outer shape of the previous cell.

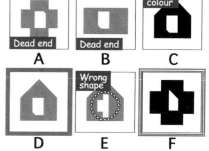

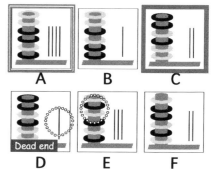 74

 Go to the next page

Answers **15, 16**

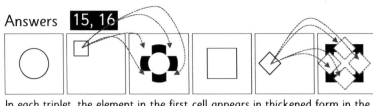

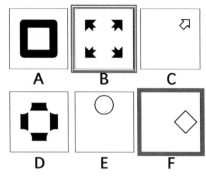

In each triplet, the element in the first cell appears in thickened form in the third cell, with four copies of the element in the second cell "bitten" out of it. The bites are in the original position of the element in the second cell, and at the 3 positions 90 degrees rotated serially around the cell. E and D would have fitted, if the circle in E was in the top left corner (instead of the middle of the top). However the diamond in F is in exactly the right place for four copies of it (including the original) to bite out the required pieces to generate B.

Answers **17, 18**

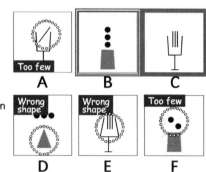

The first cell of each pair contains a shape resembling a glass with a stand. In the next cell, the upper part of the glass reappears, shaded grey and upside down, with the stand removed. Each small stick in the first cell is converted to a black disc. The arrangement of these discs is a mirror image (in a vertical mirror line) to the direction the sticks point.

Answers **19, 20**

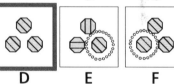

The top octagon rotates 45 degrees clockwise. The bottom left octagon rotates 45 degrees anticlockwise. The bottom right octagon rotates 90 degrees (or reflects, which is equivalent because of its symmetry.)

Answers **21, 22**

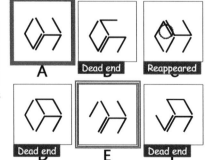

One segment of line is being removed at each step. There are several options that at first seem reasonable for the first unknown cell. However, all are "dead ends", since if they are selected there is no suitable option for the second unknown cell.

Go to the next page

Answers 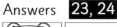 **23, 24**

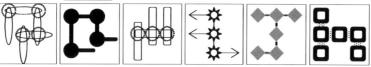

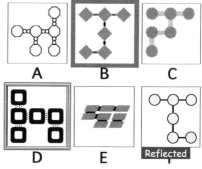

In each pair of cells, the right cell is rotated 90° anticlockwise but, apart from this, the two cells show the same pattern of connections using different symbols.

Answers **25, 26**

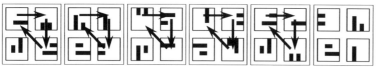

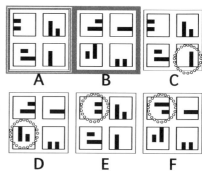

All elements rotate 90 degrees clockwise. Other than the bottom left element, the other 3 elements exchange positions by moving clockwise.

Answers **27, 28**

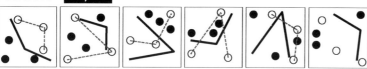

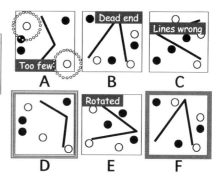

The angled pair of lines in each cell is drawn between the positions of the empty circles in the previous cell (dotted lines are now added, which makes this obvious).

Answers 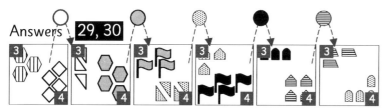 **29, 30**

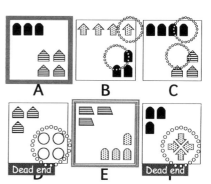

The numbers of elements remain constant: three elements in the top left area and four in the bottom right. The shape in the top left is copied into the bottom right of the next cell. The shading in the bottom right is copied into the top left of the next cell.

D and F are dead ends because if either is chosen as the 5th cell, there is no suitable option for the 6th cell.

Go to the next page ➡

Training Session 10

Congratulations, young ninja! You have attained the top level of sequence questions: 2 unknowns in 6, incorporating all sorts of rules, alone and in combination.

Apply all the skills you have learned, but keep alert for new types of rule. These core skills you have gained will help you through the other books in the Non-Verbal Ninja Training Course and, ultimately, in the exam itself.

Questions 1, 2

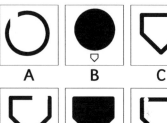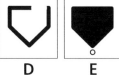

Questions 3, 4

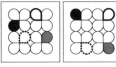

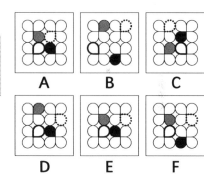

Questions 5, 6

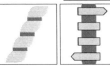

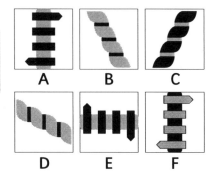

Go to the next page ➡

Questions 7, 8

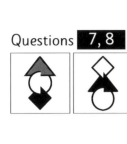 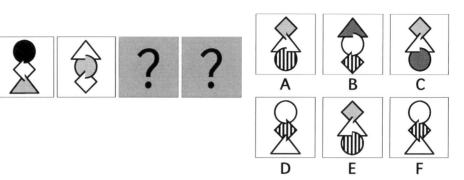

Questions 9, 10

 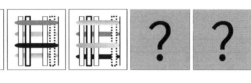 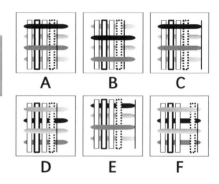

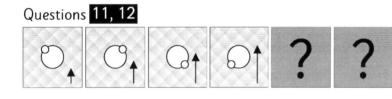 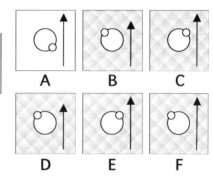

Questions 11, 12

Questions 13, 14

 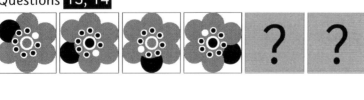 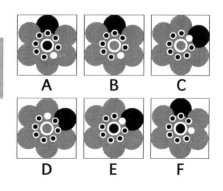

Go to the next page

Questions **15, 16**

    ? ?

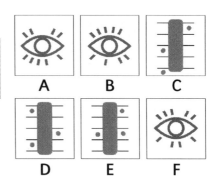

Questions **17, 18**

Questions **19, 20**

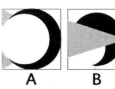
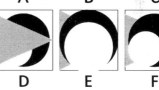

Questions **21, 22**

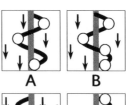
 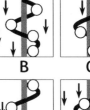

Go to the next page ▶

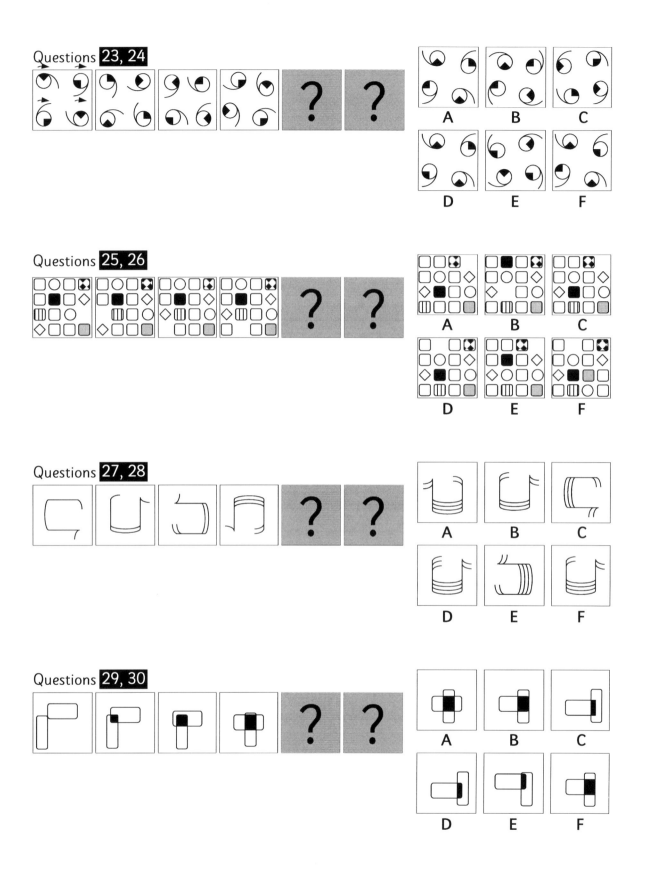

Go to the next page ➡

Answers to Session 10

Answers **1, 2**

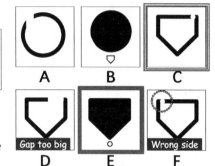

In each pair of cells, the left cell has two elements: a large upper element (shaded black) and a small lower element. The right cell is composed of an outline (unshaded) version of the upper shape, with a "bite" taken out of the right end of the top border: the bite is exactly the size of the lower element.

Answers **3, 4**

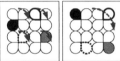

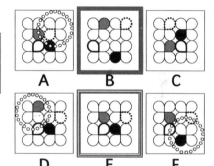

In the first (and third and fifth) step, the individual clusters of 4 leaflets rotate clockwise 90 degrees around their individual centres. In the second (and fourth) step, the whole design rotates clockwise 90 degrees.

Answers **5, 6**

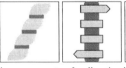

In every pair of cells, the left cell shows a diagonal piece of what might be coils of rope, with thick and thin segments. The right cell shows a vertical or horizontal bar (rotated slightly anticlockwise from the rope in the left cell) crossed by transverse strips. The major colour in the left cell becomes the colour of the bar; the minor colour in the left cell becomes the colour of the strips in the right cell.

D and F are not a solution because F is not a small **anti**clockwise rotation from D.

81

Go to the next page

Answers **7, 8**

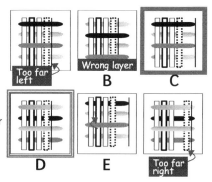

Each cell contains three elements that are interwoven as though they had slots and are slotted together like pieces of a jigsaw. In the first cell, it is as though the left side of the disc is tilted up above (closer to you than) the triangle and diamond, while the right side of the disc is below them (further away from you). There are two rules. (1) The elements move downwards at each step. The element that leaves the bottom appears at the top, but now with the opposite tilt. (2) The shading pattern moves upwards. C is a dead end because there is then no option with dark grey in the middle element.

Answers **9, 10**

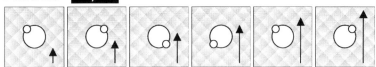

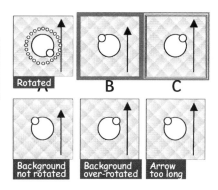

At each step the horizontal bars move down one position, with the lowest bar moving into the top position. At each step one more vertical bar moves left one position (leaving a space that seems to move to the right). Finally, the top and third horizontal bars are always in front of the vertical bars, while the second and bottom horizontal bars are always behind the vertical bars.

Answers **11, 12**

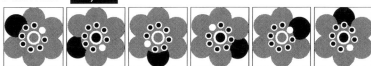

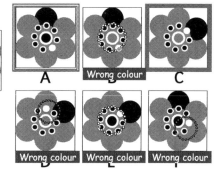

The background pattern is rotating anticlockwise. The central pattern is rotating clockwise. The arrow is progressively lengthening.

Answers **13, 14**

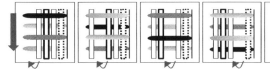

The black colouring of the outer leaf moves anticlockwise, while the white colouring of the inner disc moves clockwise two steps at a time, and the central disc alternates between grey and black.

Go to the next page ➡

Answers 15, 16

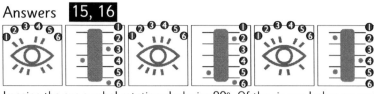

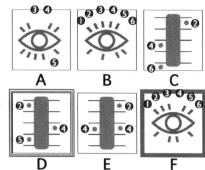

Imagine the eye symbol rotating clockwise 90°. Of the six eye lashes on each side of the eye, for each eyelash that is missing, a grey disc appears on the corresponding side in the next design.

Answers 17, 18

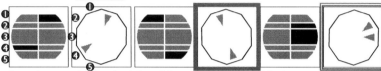

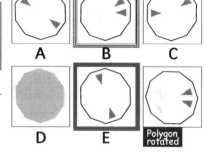

In each pair of cells, the left cell has two columns of 5 elements, while the right cell has a 10-sided shape, with a left and right half each having 5 sides. Where the left cell has an element with black shading, the right cell has a triangle associated with the corresponding side.

In the figure above, the left 5 elements and left 5 sides are numbered for in first 2 cells. Similar numbering can be done for other elements and sides.

F is incorrect because the polygon has been rotated, so there is no longer a pure vertical side at the right, and therefore no pure horizontal arrow.

Answers 19, 20

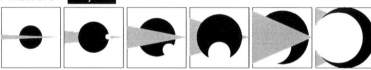

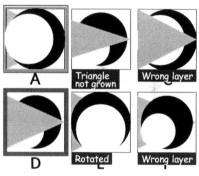

A small white disc appears on the black disc and grows progressively, moving clockwise (1/8 of a turn each step: a right angle in two steps).

Meanwhile a triangle grows in height progressively, with its horizontal centreline staying at the midlevel of the cell.

The triangle and the black-and-white disc take it in turns to be in the front layer, obscuring the other.

Answers 21, 22

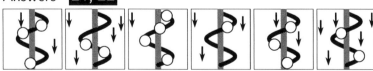

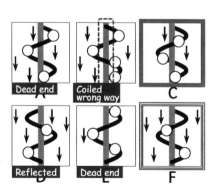

The number of white balls on the black spiral coiling around the grey pole is determined by the number of arrows in the *previous* cell. A and E are dead ends because if these are chosen, there is no correct option for the second unknown, since this would require 4 or 1 balls respectively. The 1-ball and 4-ball options are invalid and therefore the second unknown must be F, with 2 balls. Therefore you must choose the option with 2 arrows, i.e. C.

Go to the next page

Answers 23, 24

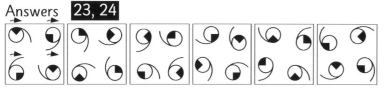

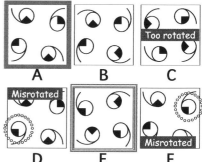

At each step, each of the four elements rotates clockwise 45 degrees.

Answers 25, 26

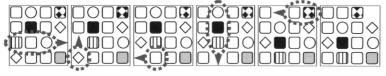

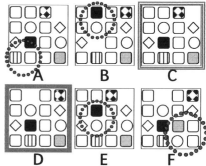

At each step, a group of one or more tiles (in a single row or column) moves together, with the leading tile moving into the space, and a new space arising at the other end of the moving group.

Answers 27, 28

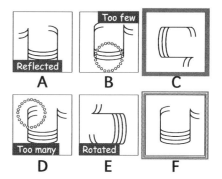

In alternate cells, either the top (joining) section gains a bar, or one of the legs gains a bar. Meanwhile the whole design is rotating anticlockwise.

Answers 29, 30

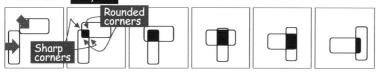

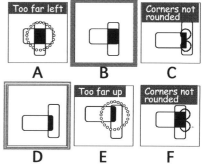

One element is moving steadily right and the other is moving steadily down. Where they overlap, the overlap region is shaded black. Because the elements are slightly rounded, the overlap regions are sometimes slightly rounded on those corners. However where the overlap region is a junction of straight sides, it is not rounded.

Go to the next page

Printed in Great Britain
by Amazon